ALL ABOUT

REPUBLICANS

 OVER 750 QUESTIONS AND ANSWERS

EDMUND LINDOP

ENSLOW PUBLISHERS, INC.

Bloy St. & Ramsey Ave.	P.O. Box 38
Box 777	Aldershot
Hillside, N.J. 07205	Hants GU12 6BP
U.S.A.	U.K.

Copyright © 1985 by Edmund Lindop

All rights reserved.

No part of this book may be reproduced by any means
without the written permission of the publisher.

Library of Congress Cataloging in Publication Data

Lindop, Edmund
  All about Republicans.

  Bibliography: p.
  Includes index.
    1. United States—Politics and government—19th century—
Miscellanea. 2. United States—Politics and government—20th
century—Miscellanea. 3. Republican Party (U.S. : 1854-   )—
Miscellanea. I. Title.
E661.L73   1985   324.2734   85-1509
ISBN 0-89490-103-6

Printed in the United States of America

10 9 8 7 6 5 4 3 2 1

CONTENTS

REPUBLICAN PRESIDENTS

1861-1865	Abraham Lincoln
1869-1877	Ulysses S. Grant
1877-1881	Rutherford B. Hayes
1881-1881	James A. Garfield
1881-1885	Chester A. Arthur
1889-1893	Benjamin Harrison
1897-1901	William McKinley
1901-1909	Theodore Roosevelt
1909-1913	William H. Taft
1921-1923	Warren G. Harding
1923-1929	Calvin Coolidge
1929-1933	Herbert Hoover
1953-1961	Dwight D. Eisenhower
1969-1974	Richard M. Nixon
1974-1977	Gerald R. Ford
1981-	Ronald Reagan

PROLOGUE:

THE BIRTH OF
THE REPUBLICAN PARTY

What great cause led to the birth of the Republican Party?

The cause of achieving freedom for *all* Americans was the cornerstone upon which a major new political party—the Republican Party—was founded in the 1850s.

What act of Congress triggered the creation of this new party?

The Kansas-Nebraska Act of 1854 permitted settlers in these two territories to vote on whether they wanted slavery. This new legislation nullified the Missouri Compromise of 1820, which had prohibited slavery north of the 36°30' parallel of latitude. Slave owners now could take over land that the Missouri Compromise had promised would forever be "free soil."

Antislavery leaders were infuriated, and they vowed to fight the extension of slavery. But they could not turn for help to the Democratic Party because it was dominated by the slaveholding South. And the Whig Party, which had effectively opposed the Democrats in the 1840s, was now in shambles. Its great leaders, Henry Clay and Daniel Webster, both were dead, and internal dissension over the slavery issue had splintered the party into warring factions. So a new party was desperately needed to advance the crusade for human freedom.

What groups of people joined to form the Republican Party?

Northern Whigs, Abolitionists, Free Soilers, and anti-slavery Democrats came together to start the new party.

When and where was the Republican Party born?

It is generally believed that the party's founders held their first meeting on February 28, 1854, at a church in Ripon, Wisconsin. This was while Congress was still debating the Kansas-Nebraska Bill, and it was decided to form a new political party if the hated bill became a law. After the Senate passed the bill and the House appeared ready to follow suit, a second meeting was held in Ripon, and a committee was appointed to organize the new party.

In July 1854, the first state convention of the infant party met in an oak grove outside the town of Jackson, Michigan. It officially adopted the name "Republican," nominated a slate of candidates for state offices, and wrote a platform denouncing slavery and demanding repeal of the Kansas-Nebraska Act.

Did the Republican Party grow quickly?

Yes. It grew faster than any new party in American history, primarily because it was a magnet that attracted people from all walks of life who shared one fundamental belief—that slavery was wrong. Rooted firmly in the Midwest, the Republican Party soon spread eastward with the speed of a prairie fire and the zeal of a religious crusade. Almost overnight it became the country's second major political party; yet it began as a purely sectional party with almost no support from the South.

When did the Republican Party run its first presidential candidate?

In 1856, just two years after its birth.

Who was the first Republican candidate for the presidency?

John Charles Frémont, the famous explorer, soldier, and California senator, was selected by the Republican convention in 1856 as its first presidential nominee.

Did Abraham Lincoln play any role at the first Republican national convention?

Yes. Lincoln (formerly a Whig) was a delegate from Illinois

and helped write the platform that denounced the extension of slavery. Lincoln was also mentioned as a candidate for the vice-presidential nomination, but an informal preliminary ballot indicated that William Dayton of New Jersey would have more than twice as many votes. So Lincoln's name was not entered in the race, and Dayton was nominated for second place on the ticket. (One wonders whether Lincoln ever would have become President if he had been on the losing Republican ticket in 1856. From a physical standpoint Frémont and Lincoln would have been an extraordinary pair of running mates—Frémont was 5 feet 2 inches tall; Lincoln was 6 feet 4 inches tall.)

How did the Republican Party do in its first presidential election?

The Republicans ran a remarkably strong race, considering that the party was only two years old and its ticket did not even appear on the ballot in 10 Southern states. In 4 other border states where slavery was permitted, Frémont's name was on the ballot, but he won only about 300 votes in each of these slave states. The Republican ticket, however, captured 11 of the 15 states in the North and Midwest, including the large states of New York, Massachusetts, and Ohio. Frémont won 114 electoral votes to 174 for James Buchanan, the victorious Democratic candidate.

What does GOP mean?

It means the Grand Old Party, which is the nickname of the Republican Party. The origin of GOP is unknown, but the term began surfacing at the Republican convention in 1880. About that time Great Britain's Prime Minister William Gladstone was fondly referred to as the Grand Old Man, and some Republican admirers of Gladstone apparently applied the same term of affection to their political party. It is ironic, however, that the Grand Old Party is more than a half century younger than the Democratic Party!

Who first publicized the elephant as the symbol of the Republican Party?

Thomas Nast, the famous political cartoonist. His caricatures of the "Republican elephant" began appearing in *Harper's Weekly* in 1874, and soon people throughout the country began associating this huge and mighty animal with the GOP.

How did the antislavery poet John Greenleaf Whittier appraise the Republicans' potential strength?

Impressed by the Republicans' surprisingly strong showing in the 1856 presidential election, Whittier wrote:

"If months have well-nigh won the field,
What may not four years do?"

Four years later, as Whittier envisioned, the party came to power with Abraham Lincoln's election as the first Republican President. And during the long period from 1861 to 1913, except for eight years, the Republicans kept their lease on the White House.

PRESIDENTS:
THEIR PERSONAL LIVES

Since 1860, when the Republican Party elected its first President, have more Republicans or Democrats occupied the White House?

Between 1860 and the end of Ronald Reagan's term of office there were 16 Republicans and 8 Democrats in the White House. The names of the Republican Presidents and the dates of their administrations are shown on page *v*. (Although Vice-President Andrew Johnson succeeded Republican Abraham Lincoln as President, Johnson was a Democrat, so he is not included with the Republican Presidents.)

Who was the only Republican President to head a labor union?

Ronald Reagan. He was elected to six one-year terms as president of the Screen Actors Guild and negotiated several contracts that provided higher wages and better pensions and medical benefits.

Did Abraham Lincoln ever see a performance by John Wilkes Booth before the tragic night when Booth assassinated him?

Yes. Lincoln watched Booth in a romantic drama called "The Marble Heart" at Ford's Theater on November 9, 1863, less than a year and a half before Booth shot him at the same theater.

Why did President James A. Garfield ask to see Abraham Lincoln's son on June 30, 1881?

President Garfield was anxious to have Robert Lincoln tell him all the details he remembered about his father's assassination. Two days after listening to Lincoln's account, Garfield became the second President to be mortally wounded by an assassin's bullet.

Who was President when the first electric lights were installed in the White House?

Benjamin Harrison. Electric lights were added to the White House in 1891, but at first the Harrisons were so afraid of this new marvel that they refused to touch the switches. Until they were convinced that the invention was safe, they went to sleep with all the lights burning.

What President's name at birth was Leslie King, Jr.?

Gerald Ford, whose mother divorced his father, Leslie King. Later she married a paint salesman named Gerald Ford, who adopted young Leslie, and the boy's name was changed to Gerald Ford, Jr.

The mother and wife of what President both died on the same day?

Theodore Roosevelt's mother and first wife both died on February 14, 1884.

What President ordered a "garage sale" of White House furniture?

Chester A. Arthur was displeased with the hodgepodge of furniture that had accumulated in the 80-year-old White House, and he refused to move in until most of it was sold and the mansion redecorated. Twenty-four wagonloads of historically priceless furniture were sold at auction, and the entire White House was redone in Victorian style by Louis Tiffany.

What future President had to resign from the army because of a serious drinking problem?

Even though he had been educated at West Point and was an officer, Ulysses S. Grant had to resign from the army because of heavy drinking. He overcame this problem and reenlisted in the army as a colonel when the Civil War started.

In a small Midwestern town what future Socialist delivered newspapers published by a conservative future President?

Ironically, when Socialist Norman Thomas was a boy, he delivered the *Marion* (Ohio) *Star*, published by Warren G. Harding.

What future President was the heavyweight wrestling champion at Yale for two years?

William H. Taft.

Dwight D. Eisenhower was proud to be a five-star general. He had his five stars displayed on what two things that were close to him?

His pajamas and his golf clubs.

What future President met his wife when they both tried out for roles in a play?

Richard Nixon met a beautiful girl named Pat Ryan at the casting of an amateur play—and proposed to her the same night. Nixon immediately won the role of a crusading district attorney in the play, but Pat stalled two years before agreeing to marry him.

A stuffed animal was named for what President?

The "teddy bear" was named for Theodore Roosevelt. On a hunting expedition to Mississippi in 1902, President Roosevelt spent four days searching in vain for a bear. Finally he spotted a cub but refused to shoot it because the bear was small and young. When reporters learned of this incident, the term "teddy bear" was born.

What President could read and write Greek, Latin, and German?

Scholarly James A. Garfield, who became a college professor and later president of Hiram College in Ohio.

Who was the only President to obtain a patent?

Abraham Lincoln was issued a patent on a "Method of Lifting Vessels over Shoals" by means of "expansible buoyant chambers."

What President was the most versatile musician?

Warren G. Harding, who boasted, "I played every instrument

except the slide trombone and the E-flat clarinet." When he was a young man, Harding played the alto horn in a band that he organized and managed in his hometown of Marion, Ohio. Harding entered the band in a statewide contest that included bands from all the large Ohio cities. He was overjoyed when his band from tiny Marion won third place.

What future President worked his way through college as a summer lifeguard?

Ronald Reagan was a lifeguard at a beach on the Rock River near his hometown of Dixon, Illinois. He held this $18-a-week job during his last three years of high school and four years of college, and over this seven-year span he rescued about 80 persons from drowning. (Reagan earned additional money for college as a dishwasher in a fraternity house.)

What college did Ronald Reagan attend?

Eureka College, a small Christian Church college in Illinois, 60 miles from his home.

What were Reagan's chief college activities?

He played guard on the football team, captained the swimming team, participated in campus dramatics, was a member of the debate team, worked on the yearbook, and served as a student council officer.

Who was the first President to ride in an automobile?

William McKinley, who took his first ride in a Stanley Steamer in 1899.

Who was the first President to do both these things—ride to his inauguration in an automobile and give his inaugural address over the radio?

Warren G. Harding, in 1921.

Who was the son of one President and the father of another President?

John Harrison was the son of Whig President William Henry Harrison and the father of Republican President Benjamin Harrison. Although he never reached the White House himself,

John Harrison was a two-term congressman. He also attained some macabre fame posthumously. In 1878 Harrison's body was stolen from its grave by "cadaver kidnappers," who sold it to the Ohio Medical College for students to dissect. When it was discovered who the dead man was, a storm of indignation swept the country, and laws were passed that gave severe penalties to grave robbers.

The night before his inauguration, what President prepared for this grueling occasion by boxing ten rounds with a former middleweight champion?

Theodore Roosevelt boxed with Mike Donovan on March 3, 1905, the evening before his inauguration for a full four-year term in the White House. "Now, Mike," cautioned Roosevelt when the two boxers stepped on the mat, "we must have a good bout this evening. It will brighten me for tomorrow, which will be a trying day."

Why did Roosevelt's boxing in the White House come to a sudden end?

When a young army boxer landed a blow that caused Roosevelt to lose the sight of his left eye, the President gave up boxing. This accident, however, did not end Roosevelt's zeal for rough contact sports. He turned instead to wrestling and jujitsu.

Who never drew his salary as President, donating the money instead to charities?

Millionaire Herbert Hoover.

What Republican President was born in Texas?

Dwight D. Eisenhower was born in Denison, Texas.

What former President fathered a child when he was nearly 64?

Benjamin Harrison's second wife bore him a daughter in 1897, four years after he left the White House. Harrison had four grandchildren who were older than this daughter.

What Republican President had the longest life?

Herbert Hoover, who lived 90 years and 72 days. Of all our Presidents, Hoover lived longer than any other except John Adams, whose life spanned 90 years and 247 days.

What future President was such a fine horseman that he set a West Point record for jumping that stood for 25 years?

Ulysses S. Grant.

What President-elect barely escaped death on the trip to his inauguration?

In February 1861, Abraham Lincoln traveled by train from his home in Springfield, Illinois, to Washington, D.C. Conspirators plotted to kill the President-elect when his train reached the depot in Baltimore, Maryland. But the plot was uncovered, so Lincoln was persuaded to leave his train secretly at Philadelphia and ride into Washington in a different, heavily guarded railroad car.

What former President barely escaped death or serious injury on the trip home after leaving the White House?

Former President Rutherford B. Hayes left Washington by train after attending the inauguration of his successor, James A. Garfield, in 1881. Near Baltimore his train collided with another. Two passengers on Hayes's train were killed, and 20 others were badly injured. Hayes was thrown several feet out of his seat, but he was not hurt.

What President's son died from a foot infection that occurred while he was playing tennis on the White House court?

Calvin Coolidge, Jr., who died at age 16 on July 7, 1924. His father wrote in his autobiography that after young Calvin's death the power and glory of the presidency no longer were meaningful to him.

What President was named for a great-grandfather who had signed the Declaration of Independence?

Benjamin Harrison, whose great-grandfather was a portly colonist from Virginia.

Who was the student manager of the first Stanford football team?

Herbert Hoover. In 1892 he made all the arrangements for the Far West's first intercollegiate football game between the new school called Stanford and the University of California.

Hoover purchased the players' uniforms on credit, supplied the football, and collected the gate receipts. Stanford upset the team from Berkeley, 14-10, and that was the beginning of a great traditional rivalry which even today is called "The Big Game."

What President wore a white vest and a red carnation in his buttonhole nearly every day?

William McKinley.

What President started the tradition of throwing out the first ball to launch the major league baseball season?

William H. Taft, an avid baseball fan, inaugurated this annual custom in 1910.

What GOP President was especially fond of the Southerners' favorite song, "Dixie"?

Abraham Lincoln, who first heard the song at a minstrel show in 1860. Shortly after the Civil War ended, Lincoln declared, "I have always thought 'Dixie' was one of the best tunes I ever heard." Then the President whimsically added, "I have heard that our adversaries over the way had attempted to appropriate it. I insisted yesterday that we had fairly captured it."

Our heaviest President was a Republican. Who was he?

William H. Taft, who tipped the scales at between 330 and 350 pounds. He required a special oversize bathtub, and when Taft played golf he had difficulty tucking his stomach in far enough to see the ball.

What musical instrument did Abraham Lincoln play in his youth?

Lincoln played the mouth harp, a lyre-shaped instrument held between the teeth and played by striking the free metal end with a finger. Shortly after his election to the presidency, Lincoln wrote to a musical society: "Many persons now are busy trying to ascertain what our next President delighted in during his younger days. I will tell you confidentially that my greatest pleasure when taking a rest after splitting rails was to play a solo on the Jew's-harp [mouth harp]. Now keep this to yourself."

What President enjoyed skiing so much that he bought a place in Colorado so that he could ski during winter vacations?

Gerald Ford, who bought a condominium at Vail, Colorado.

What President had a "Tennis Cabinet"?

Theodore Roosevelt, who often played a vigorous game of tennis with government aides. The President had an unusual way of serving a tennis ball. Instead of tossing it over his head, Roosevelt hit the ball while still holding it between the fingers of his left hand.

One of the Republican Presidents enjoyed painting as a hobby. Who was he?

Dwight D. Eisenhower.

Who was the last President born in a log cabin?

James A. Garfield, who was born in 1831.

As a youth what musical talents did Richard Nixon display?

Nixon started playing the piano at age seven, and his mother hoped he would become a professional pianist. When her son was 12, she sent him to live for a while with an aunt who was an excellent piano teacher. Nixon's aunt was so pleased with his progress that she predicted he could become a superb musician. In high school and college Nixon continued his piano studies. He also played second violin in his high school orchestra and sang in his college glee club.

In what small town was Abraham Lincoln a store clerk and postmaster?

In New Salem, Illinois.

What position in football did Gerald Ford play?

Gerald Ford was the center on a team at South High School in Grand Rapids, Michigan, that won the state championship in his senior year. He played the same position at the University of Michigan. Following his senior year, Ford was honored as Michigan's Most Valuable Player and selected as the center on the Big-10's All-Conference Team.

What President, formerly an army general, despised hunting and

never could kill an animal or bird?

Ulysses S. Grant.

What twentieth-century President often swam nude in the Potomac River?

Theodore Roosevelt.

What Republican President had served as the head of a large eastern university?

Dwight D. Eisenhower was appointed president of Columbia University in June 1948, and held that position until he became the first commander of NATO forces in Europe in December 1950.

What President played a strenuous game of medicine ball with government officials every day except Sunday?

Herbert Hoover, whose exercising companions were called the "Medicine-Ball Cabinet." A medicine ball is larger and heavier than a basketball, and the game consisted of throwing it back and forth vigorously.

What future President once played the role of the heroine, Desdemona, in Shakespeare's *Othello*?

In 1845 when Ulysses S. Grant was a young lieutenant stationed at Corpus Christi, Texas, he and his army buddies decided to perform some of Shakespeare's plays. Since there were no women in camp, some of the soldiers had to play female roles. Grant, who had rosy cheeks and deep blue eyes, was cast as Desdemona, and in this role he wore a bell-shaped skirt and carried a dainty fan.

What two Presidents enjoyed old-fashioned Sunday night hymn-sings in the White House?

Rutherford B. Hayes and William McKinley. When Hayes was President he invited Congressman McKinley to these Sunday songfests; McKinley liked the custom so much that he resumed it when he became Chief Executive.

The son of what President took a pet pony up the White House elevator to cheer his young brother who was ill with measles?

Quentin, one of Theodore Roosevelt's four sons, brought the pony up to brother Archie's room.

Where did Abraham Lincoln often carry important government papers?

In the crown of his stovepipe hat.

What future President was embarrassed because his father had to accompany him to get his marriage license?

Benjamin Harrison, who was only 20 at the time. Since Harrison was a minor, his father had to appear with him at the licensing office and give his approval before the license could be issued.

Horatio Alger, famous for his rags-to-riches stories, wrote about whom in his biography, *From Canal Boy to President*?

This biography was about James A. Garfield, who as a poor, fatherless youth, drove teams of horses that drew barges along the Ohio canals.

What President was assassinated at a Pan-American Exposition in Buffalo?

On September 6, 1901, William McKinley was standing in a receiving line, shaking hands with visitors to the Exposition. Just after the President had given the red carnation from his buttonhole to a little girl, anarchist Leon Czolgosz approached him. Czolgosz's hand was covered by a handkerchief that looked like a bandage but concealed a gun. The assassin shot McKinley twice before he was grabbed by the police. Eight days later the President died.

What future President had his first book published two years after he left college?

Theodore Roosevelt started writing *The Naval War of 1812* while a student at Harvard, and the book was published two years later in 1882. Some of his other books (which numbered almost 40) were *Winning of the West, African Game Trails,* and his autobiography.

What President won the Ben Hogan Trophy for being the golfer whose recovery from a physical ailment most inspired other golfers?

Dwight D. Eisenhower won this award in 1956, after recovering from his first heart attack.

What dignified President rescued his small grandson when the goat that was pulling his wagon started racing wildly down Pennsylvania Avenue?

Benjamin Harrison.

What President was so devoted to his frail wife that after he had been mortally wounded by an assassin's bullet, the only thing he said was, "My wife, be careful how you tell her—oh, be careful"?

William McKinley.

What future President played the title role in "Sleeping Beauty" at a church benefit?

Of all persons, big, beefy William H. Taft performed the role of Sleeping Beauty. Helen Herron, who at that time was his girl friend and later his wife, recalled that Taft's burlesque portrayal of the delicate heroine was "a huge success."

What sons of Republican Presidents served in the Cabinets of other Presidents?

Robert T. Lincoln was Secretary of War under Presidents Garfield and Arthur. James R. Garfield was Secretary of the Interior in Theodore Roosevelt's administration.

What President smoked about twenty cigars a day?

Ulysses S. Grant, who developed throat cancer.

Who made the first presidential telephone call?

Rutherford B. Hayes. In 1877 he spoke on the phone with inventor Alexander Graham Bell over a distance of 13 miles. A short time later Hayes had the first telephone installed in the White House. But it was not until 1929, during the Hoover administration, that the first phone sat on the desk of a President.

Which of the assassinated Presidents lived for over two months after he was shot?

James A. Garfield was shot on July 2, 1881, and lived until September 19.

How did Alexander Graham Bell try to save President Garfield's life?

Doctors were unable to locate the bullet that lodged inside Garfield's body, so they summoned inventor Bell to the President's bedside because he had recently built an electric metal detector. But when Bell used his invention on Garfield, the machine recorded continuous contact with metal, so it was of no value to the President's doctors. Later it was discovered why Bell's invention could not locate the bullet. Garfield had been lying on a spring mattress, and its metal coils caused the machine to malfunction.

What future President was described by *The New York Times* as "one of the most promising backs in Eastern football"?

Dwight D. Eisenhower, who was left halfback on the 1912 Army team. When Army faced the Carlisle Indians, led by the legendary Jim Thorpe, Eisenhower played brilliantly on both offense and defense. But in that game he wrenched a knee, and his playing days were over. Even so, his football career was so spectacular that his name was imprinted on a bronze tablet in the West Point gymnasium alongside tablets with the names of other great Army athletes.

What President married the niece of his first wife?

After his first wife died, Benjamin Harrison married her niece, Mary Dimmick.

What President's son once rode his bicycle down the main staircase of the White House?

James A. Garfield's son Abram.

What President's son once startled White House guests by driving his pet goats hitched to a kitchen chair through the formal East Room?

Abraham Lincoln's son Tad.

Who was the youngest President at the time that he entered the White House?

Theodore Roosevelt, who was 42 when he was elevated to the presidency after the death of William McKinley.

Who was the oldest President at the time that he entered the White House?

Ronald Reagan, who was 69 when he was inaugurated on January 20, 1981, and turned 70 the following February 6.

Next to Ronald Reagan, who was the oldest President at the time that he left the White House?

Dwight D. Eisenhower, whose age was 70 years and 98 days when he completed the second term of his presidency.

So that he could leave his family without a huge debt, what former President wrote his memoirs while dying from cancer?

Ulysses S. Grant, who had contracted a huge debt in a disastrous Wall Street venture following his presidency. Even though he endured great pain, Grant kept writing until the project was completed, about one week before his death. His memoirs provided about $450,000 to pay off his debt.

Before he became President and faced worse crises, who wrote a book called *My Six Crises*?

Richard Nixon.

What President was a mining engineer?

Herbert Hoover, whose profession took him to five continents and made him a huge fortune.

About what President did the legendary boxer John L. Sullivan say, "The Creator played a low-down trick on the Irish when He made him a Dutchman"?

Sullivan said this about Theodore Roosevelt, who was his close friend. When Roosevelt set out on his expedition to Africa after he left the White House, Sullivan gave him a gold-mounted rabbit's foot, which the former President carried for luck throughout the journey.

What future President gained the respect of a hard-fighting gang known as the Clary's Grove boys when he outwrestled their leader, Jack Armstrong?

Abraham Lincoln.

Who was the first President to have been divorced?

Ronald Reagan. His eight-year marriage to film actress Jane Wyman (who won an Academy Award for her performance in *Johnny Belinda*) ended in a divorce in 1948.

One son died in World War I, and two other sons died in World War II. What President was their father?

Theodore Roosevelt. His son Quentin was killed in World War I, and later his sons Theodore, Jr. and Kermit died while on active duty in World War II.

Which state is the birthplace of the largest number of Republican Presidents?

Ohio is the birthplace of seven GOP Presidents—Grant, Hayes, Garfield, Harrison, McKinley, Taft, and Harding. Virginia is the birthplace of eight Presidents, but none was a Republican.

Where was Gerald Ford born?

In Omaha, Nebraska.

On the day of his assassination what eerie dream did Abraham Lincoln describe to his Cabinet?

Lincoln said that in a dream (the night before his death) he saw himself "floating in an undescribable vessel and moving rapidly toward an indistinct shore."

What President said, "I only know two tunes—one of them is 'Yankee Doodle' and the other isn't"?

Ulysses S. Grant.

What President invented an "obstacle walk" for hiking parties that he organized?

Theodore Roosevelt decided where the starting and ending points of his long hikes would be, and he insisted that all his companions cover the distance by walking in a straight line. This might include climbing rocks, jumping over gulleys, swimming across streams, and swinging from tree branches, but Roosevelt's friends felt honored to accompany the President on his "obstacle walks."

Whose wife died the year before he became President?

Chester A. Arthur's wife Ellen. When she died at 42, her husband ordered that her room never be touched again.

Who was Chester A. Arthur's hostess at the White House?

His sister Mary McElroy.

The sons of what two Presidents followed in their father's footsteps by graduating from West Point?

Ulysses S. Grant's son Frederick and Dwight D. Eisenhower's son John.

What two professional football teams offered Gerald Ford contracts?

Both the Detroit Lions and the Green Bay Packers offered Ford contracts, but he turned them down to take a job as assistant football coach at Yale. While Ford was at Yale he earned his law degree and began developing an interest in politics.

What future President insisted that a former President pay for his ticket to a college baseball game?

Herbert Hoover was the student manager of the Stanford baseball (as well as the football) team, and he was upset when the ticket taker allowed former President Benjamin Harrison to enter the baseball park without paying. So Hoover walked over to the distinguished guest and got him to buy a ticket, which cost 25 cents.

How many of Abraham Lincoln's four sons grew to manhood?

Only one, Robert Todd, who lived to be 82 and died in 1926. Edward died in infancy, and Thomas "Tad" died at age 18. William "Willie" died in the White House when he was 11, and Mrs. Lincoln was so grief-stricken that she never again entered the room where Willie passed away.

Who was the first President to have "The White House" printed on his stationery as the return address?

Theodore Roosevelt. Before his administration the Executive Mansion often was unofficially called the White House, but it was also known as the President's Palace and the President's House.

Who was the first left-handed President?

James A. Garfield.

What President got a ticket for speeding?

Ulysses S. Grant was ticketed by a Washington mounted policeman for exceeding the speed limit—in a buggy hitched to a team of fast trotters.

What President had been a Western cowboy who herded wild horses, lassoed stubborn steers, and rode bucking broncos?

Theodore Roosevelt, who lived a strenuous life on the ranch he owned in the Badlands of the Dakota Territory.

What President had seven sons?

Rutherford B. Hayes, who was a devoted family man. When he and his wife celebrated their 25th wedding anniversary in the White House, they repeated their marriage vows.

What President usually kept his White House guests at the dinner table for two to three hours?

Chester A. Arthur. He was both a lonely widower and a connoisseur of gourmet food, so his dinner parties were among the longest in White House history.

What future President was orphaned before he was ten years old?

Herbert Hoover, whose father died when he was six and whose mother died when he was nine. After the death of both parents, Hoover left his hometown of West Branch, Iowa, and lived with an aunt and uncle in Oregon.

What future President was one of the champion runners at Kenyon College?

Rutherford B. Hayes.

What President's son became president of Williams College?

James A. Garfield's son Harry.

What was similar about the two attempts to assassinate President Gerald Ford?

Both attempts were made by women carrying guns. They both occurred in California within a 17-day period in the fall of 1975.

What President had a river in South America named for him?

Theodore Roosevelt, who explored parts of the Amazon tropical rain forest on his last expedition in 1914. For about six weeks he traveled down the raging River of Doubt, with its dangerous rapids and sharp-edged boulders. Because Roosevelt led the first party of white explorers to navigate a large stretch of this wild river, its name was changed to Rio Roosevelt.

When he was a teenager, what future President had his name changed by a congressman?

Ulysses S. Grant was christened Hiram Ulysses Grant, but as a youth he was called by his middle name. So the congressman who recommended him for West Point assumed that his first name was Ulysses and his middle was Simpson because that was the name of his mother's family. Hiram Ulysses Grant was enrolled at West Point as Ulysses Simpson Grant, and that became his name for the rest of his life.

A reporter described what President-elect as having a high-pitched voice, unprepossessing features, the gawkiest figure, and the most awkward manners?

Abraham Lincoln.

The granite portraits of what two Republican Presidents are among the four carved at Mount Rushmore, South Dakota?

Abraham Lincoln and Theodore Roosevelt.

What future President was the youngest of all the Republican Vice-Presidents?

Richard Nixon, who was 40 at the time of his inauguration.

What President felt ashamed because his father had hired a substitute soldier, rather than be drafted, during the Civil War?

Theodore Roosevelt. It was a common practice among many wealthy men in New York to avoid being drafted in the Civil War by paying substitutes to take their place. But Theodore Roosevelt harbored a feeling of shame because his father had been one of these draft dodgers. This may partly explain Teddy's compulsion to lead a rugged life and his overwhelming desire to fight in the Spanish-American War and World War I.

What former President was the honored guest at an 8-hour, 70-course dinner?

While he was on a two-year global tour, Ulysses S. Grant was served this dinner by a Chinese government official. There is no mention of how Grant's stomach felt following this marathon meal.

How did Camp David get its name?

This famous presidential retreat in Maryland, scene of the Israeli-Egyptian agreement in President Carter's administration, was named by President Eisenhower for his grandson David.

What President's daughter married a future Speaker of the House and reigned as the grand dame of Washington society for many years?

Theodore Roosevelt's eldest daughter, Alice. In 1906 "Princess Alice," as the newspapers called her, was married in a White House wedding to Congressman Nicholas Longworth, who later became Speaker of the House. Combining elegance and charm with a caustic wit, Mrs. Longworth reigned over Washington society for two thirds of a century. She made her home in the capital until she died at age 96 in 1980.

Who was the daughter of one President and the wife of another President's grandson?

Julie Nixon Eisenhower, the daughter of Richard Nixon and the wife of Dwight D. Eisenhower's grandson David.

What Republican President fathered an illegitimate daughter?

Warren G. Harding. His mistress, Nan Britton, had been a high school reporter for the newspaper Harding published in Marion, Ohio. Although Harding was old enough to be her father, Nan fell hopelessly in love with the handsome publisher-politician, who at first regarded her affection as a teenager's infatuation. But after Harding moved to Washington as a senator in 1915, Nan went to New York and contacted him for help in finding a job. Harding visited her—then a 20-year-old beautiful blonde—and they began an affair. Later their child was conceived, allegedly on a couch in Harding's Senate office.

Did this affair continue after Harding became President?

Yes. Their favorite hideaway was a small coat closet next to the President's office. The affair, however, was not known to the public until four years after Harding's death, when Nan Britton wrote a sensational best-seller, *The President's Daughter.*

Did Harding have any other extramarital love affairs?

Yes. Long before Nan Britton became his mistress, Harding was involved with Carrie Phillips, a woman in his hometown who happened to be one of his wife's best friends. Their affair lasted about 15 years, but it was a well-kept secret until the 1960s when many of their handwritten love letters were discovered.

Who earned nearly $500,000 in royalties for a book he wrote about his experiences before he became President?

Dwight D. Eisenhower, whose 1949 book *Crusade in Europe*, told of his experiences as the Supreme Commander of Allied Forces in World War II.

What former President gathered one of the world's largest collections of East African animals?

Theodore Roosevelt returned from his African safari with 296 stuffed animals of 70 different species, which were given to the Smithsonian Institution in Washington, D.C.

What future President was for five years a sportscaster for a radio station in Des Moines, Iowa?

Ronald Reagan. He provided live coverage of Big Ten football games and track meets, and he did simulated broadcasts of Chicago Cubs' baseball games from a Western Union ticker. Once the ticker broke down just as the Cubs' Augie Galan came to bat. Reagan decided to improvise—so he described Galan hitting one imaginary foul ball after another—for six long minutes until the ticker started again, and then he resumed the true account of the game.

How did sports announcer Ronald Reagan become a movie star?

In 1937 he accompanied the Chicago Cubs to their spring training camp in southern California, where a friend introduced him to a casting director who gave Reagan a screen test. The handsome 26-year-old sportscaster passed the test with flying colors, signed a $200-a-week contract with Warner Brothers, and made his first film, *Love Is on the Air*, in which he was cast in the familiar role of a radio announcer.

What two famous athletes did Reagan portray in the movies?

He played the part of Notre Dame football star George Gipp in *Knute Rockne—All American* (1940). Gipp's tragic death in the film gave rise to the emotion-charged plea, "Win this one for the Gipper!" Later Reagan portrayed the ailing Hall of Fame pitcher Grover Cleveland Alexander in *The Winning Team* (1952).

Did Ronald Reagan ever win an Academy Award?

No, but in 1942 he starred in *King's Row*, a film that was nominated for an Oscar as the Best Motion Picture. The future President portrayed a small-town playboy who loses both his legs. Reagan felt that *King's Row* was the best of the 54 movies he made in a film career that spanned nearly 30 years.

How did Reagan get the title of his 1965 autobiography, *Where's the Rest of Me?*

In the role he played in *King's Row*, Reagan cried out in horror, "Where's the rest of me?" This occurred when he discovered that his legs had been amputated by an insane surgeon.

How did Reagan's Hollywood image probably help him at the polls?

In his film career he portrayed a long list of "good guys," and the public's favorable perception of Reagan, the actor, could easily have helped Reagan, the candidate.

In the movies did Reagan ever play the part of a villain?

Only once. In his final film, *The Killers,* (1964), Reagan was cast as the head of a criminal ring who was murdered by one of his own hired assassins.

Why have Reagan's old films rarely been shown on TV in recent election years?

Because the Federal Communications Commission ruled in 1976 that rerunning old Reagan movies, even those in which he had only minor roles, could be legitimately challenged by political opponents who demanded equal time on TV.

Did Reagan's acting career include television, as well as movies?

Yes. From 1954 until 1962 he was the host and occasional

star of the popular weekly TV show *General Electric Theater*, and after he left this program he served for two years as host of another television show, *Death Valley Days.*

Since Reagan has long been identified with the movie and TV industries, is his California home in Hollywood?

No. For many years Reagan had a hillside home at 1669 San Onofre Drive in Pacific Palisades, about 10 miles west of Hollywood. But his favorite hideaway is his 688-acre ranch, called "Rancho del Cielo," in the Santa Ynez Mountains. Near Santa Barbara, Reagan's ranch is about 100 miles north of Los Angeles. On this ranch he keeps horses and cattle.

Five Presidents, including Ronald Reagan, were shot by would-be assassins. How many of them survived?

Only Reagan survived, even though he was older than any of the Presidents who were assassinated.

What former All-American football player is President Reagan's minister?

Dr. Donn Moomaw, who was an All-American lineman at UCLA, and is the minister at the Bel-Air Presbyterian Church in west Los Angeles.

What are Reagan's favorite forms of recreation?

He likes to chop firewood and clear the brush at his ranch. But most of all, he enjoys horseback riding, staying in the saddle for two or three hours at a time. One of Reagan's favorite quotations is: "There's nothing so good for the inside of a man as the outside of a horse."

About how many guests did President and Mrs. Reagan entertain during their first three years in the Executive Mansion?

The total number of guests was 222,758.

In 1984 Reagan wrote an article for the Sunday newspaper supplement *Parade*, telling how he stayed fit in the White House. What was included in his health regimen?

The President said he worked out with weights and on a treadmill for 25 minutes a day in the exercise room and swam often in the White House pool. He followed a diet that was light, lean, and almost salt-free. "I mean," he explained, "you'd have to be a racoon or something to eat a hard-boiled egg without salt, but I use very little."

Has Reagan grown much heavier or taller since his college days?

When Reagan entered college he weighed 175 pounds and was 6 feet tall; now he weighs about 185 pounds and stands 6 feet, 1 inch. However, he had a big growth spurt in high school. In 1927, when he started high school Reagan weighed only about 108 pounds, and his height was 5 feet, 3 inches.

What was the occupation of Reagan's father?

He was a shoe salesman.

What was the religious background of Reagan's parents?

His father was a Catholic, and his mother belonged to the Christian (Disciples of Christ) Church.

When the Reagans bought their ranch near Santa Barbara, did it have a modern farm house?

No, the main house was a ninety-year-old adobe building.

What head of state braved a raging rainstorm and rode many miles over a slippery, bumpy dirt road to visit the Reagans at their ranch in 1983?

Queen Elizabeth of Great Britain.

President and Mrs. Reagan spent several days in 1984 in what Communist country?

China.

Ronald Reagan has had three careers—a sports announcer, a Hollywood actor, and, beginning at age 55, a politician. How does he compare these three careers?

In a letter to his son, Reagan said, "When I was announcing sports I was happy and thought that was all I wanted out of life. Then came the chance at Hollywood, and that was even better. Now I'm doing something that makes everything else I've done seem dull as dishwater."

PRESIDENTS:
THEIR PUBLIC CAREERS

Who was the first President to appoint a woman justice to the Supreme Court?

Ronald Reagan. In July 1981, he named Sandra Day O'Connor of Arizona to fill a vacancy on the Supreme Court. Mrs. O'Connor had been the first woman to serve as a majority leader of a state legislature, and since 1979 she had been a judge in the Arizona State Court of Appeals.

Was Ronald Reagan elected to any political offices before he was elected governor of California in 1966?

No.

Who was the last Republican governor, before Ronald Reagan, to become President?

Governor Calvin Coolidge of Massachusetts, who became President when Harding died in 1923 and was elected to a full four-year term in 1924.

When did former Democrat Reagan first attract the attention of Republican leaders?

Ronald Reagan, who had changed his voter registration from Democrat to Republican in 1962, first impressed Republican leaders as an up-and-coming new star in their party when he made a superb speech supporting Barry Goldwater's 1964 campaign for the presidency.

When Reagan became governor, he inherited a budget deficit of $194 million. When he left office, was California still in debt?

No. When Reagan completed his tenure as governor, the California treasury had a surplus of $554 million.

As governor of California was Reagan able to hold down the size of the government bureaucracy?

Yes. During Reagan's eight years as governor the number of full-time state employees rose less than 6,000 from the 102,000 who were on the government payroll when he took office.

How did Governor Reagan reform the welfare program in California?

He tightened eligibility requirements, which cut the number of welfare recipients by about 400,000, while increasing the benefits for the truly needy people by about 40 percent. Governor Reagan also imposed work requirements on welfare recipients who were able to hold jobs.

Did Governor Reagan support any measures to improve the environment?

Yes. He signed two of the strongest air- and water-pollution laws in the country. He established an air-resources board and gave it the power to enforce rigid standards. By executive directive Governor Reagan initiated the concept of environmental impact studies on new construction in the state. He also set aside 145,000 acres of park lands, including 41 miles of valuable oceanfront.

It has been said that a Republican President cannot work well with a Democratic Congress because he uses his veto power too often. Do Republican Presidents generally veto more bills than Democratic Presidents?

No. The three Presidents who vetoed the most bills were all Democrats. Franklin D. Roosevelt vetoed 635 bills, Grover Cleveland 614, and Harry S Truman 250. Republican Richard Nixon used his veto power only 42 times, and Republican Gerald Ford 66 times.

How many Republican Presidents completed two full terms in the White House?

Surprisingly, only two of the 16 Republican Presidents completed two full terms in the White House. They were Ulysses S. Grant (1869-1877) and Dwight D. Eisenhower (1953-1961).

What President proclaimed, "This is the greatest week in the history of the world since creation"?

Richard Nixon said this when our astronauts first landed on the moon in July 1969.

Who was the only American to hold the highest offices in both the executive and judicial branches of our government?

William Howard Taft, who was President (1909-1913) and Chief Justice of the Supreme Court (1921-1930).

What Republican became President in the same election in which Anagnostopoulous and Marciszewski were the vice-presidential candidates of the two major parties?

Richard Nixon was elected President in the 1968 election in which Anagnostopoulous and Marciszewski were vice-presidential candidates. Fortunately for the political careers of their ambitious descendants, the Greek Anagnostopoulous family changed its name to Agnew and the Polish Marciszewski family changed its name to Muskie.

What three Republicans never were elected to a public office before they became Presidents?

Ulysses S. Grant, Herbert Hoover, and Dwight D. Eisenhower.

Who was the only Republican to serve in the House of Representatives, the Senate, the vice-presidency, and the presidency?

Richard Nixon, who was a congressman from 1947 to 1951, a senator from 1951 to 1953, Vice-President from 1953 to 1961, and President from 1969 to 1974.

What Republican Presidents had been officers in the armed forces?

Abraham Lincoln was a captain of volunteers who fought Indians in the Black Hawk War. Four future Presidents were field generals in the Civil War—Grant, Hayes, Garfield, and

Harrison. Arthur during the Civil War was quartermaster-general in New York City, a responsible position in which he supplied housing, equipment, and food for the thousands of Union troops who passed through the city. McKinley was a major in the Civil War, and his successor in the White House, Theodore Roosevelt, was a much-publicized lieutenant colonel in the Spanish-American War. Eisenhower was a five-star general in World War II. Both Nixon and Ford were in the Navy and served in the Pacific theater. They both rose through the ranks and became lieutenant commanders. During World War II Ronald Reagan was a captain in the Air Force who narrated training films.

Who was the only President to be preceded and succeeded in the White House by the same man?

Benjamin Harrison, who was President between Grover Cleveland's terms. The only President who served two nonconsecutive terms was Cleveland.

What Republican President won the Nobel Peace Prize?

Theodore Roosevelt won the Nobel Peace Prize for negotiating the peace treaty that ended the Russo-Japanese War in 1905.

When Lincoln was elected President in 1860, who was elected Vice-President?

Senator Hannibal Hamlin of Maine. Lincoln had never even met Hamlin until after the Republican convention nominated him for second place on the ticket.

What future President was nominated for Congress without his consent and elected without his campaigning?

Rutherford B. Hayes. He was fighting in the Civil War when his friends back home nominated and elected him to Congress, but he refused to take his seat until after the war ended. Hayes had enlisted in the army as a private and rose to the rank of major general. He was wounded in battle five times and had four horses shot out from under him.

What future President headed a relief commission that helped feed and clothe the Belgian people during World War I?

Herbert Hoover.

Was President Nixon's action unprecedented when he tried to reject court subpoenas to turn over tapes in the Watergate case?

No. In 1807 Chief Justice John Marshall issued a subpoena to President Thomas Jefferson to release a letter sought by defense attorneys in Aaron Burr's treason case. President Jefferson refused to comply with the subpoena, asserting that "the leading principle of our Constitution is the independence of the legislature, executive, and judiciary of each other...but would the executive be independent of the judiciary if he were subject to the commands of the latter and to imprisonment for disobedience?" The question of whether a President can be forced to comply with a subpoena was not tested in the Burr case because President Jefferson finally agreed to make most of the subpoenaed letter available to the court.

Another Democratic President, James Monroe, was subpoenaed to testify at a court-martial. President Monroe refused to appear in court, but he answered written questions from the court.

What wartime President appeared uninvited before a Senate committee to deny that any member of his family held "treasonable communication with the enemy"?

Abraham Lincoln. In 1863, when the Civil War was going badly for the Union forces, congressional leaders speculated that Mrs. Lincoln, who came from a Southern family, might be spying for the South. The question of treason was such a grave matter that President Lincoln felt compelled to go before the Senate committee investigating this charge and declare emphatically that it was not true.

How did President Gerald Ford react when the Cambodian Communists seized the American merchant ship *Mayaguez*, in May 1975?

He ordered air strikes against the Cambodian mainland and the landing of Marines at Tang Island. The 39 *Mayaguez* crewmen were quickly released.

What President used his office to help save the sport of college football?

Theodore Roosevelt. He was deeply concerned because in the first five years of this century 45 players were killed and several hundred were severely injured in college football games. So in 1905 President Roosevelt invited to a Washington conference the athletic officials from major Eastern colleges where football was played. He warned them "to make the game of football a rather less homicidal pastime," or it would disappear from the American sport scene. The college leaders took the President's advice, and the following year they started adopting new rules that made the game safer.

What President was administered the oath of office by his father?

Calvin Coolidge was sworn in as President by his father, who was a notary public. The simple ceremony was held at Coolidge's birthplace in Plymouth, Vermont, shortly after he received word of President Harding's death.

Who said about the presidency: "In this job I'm not worried about my enemies. It's my friends who are keeping me awake nights"?

Warren G. Harding, who had reason to feel this way when he found out about Teapot Dome and other scandals instigated by his friends.

What key position in Congress did Gerald Ford hold at the time he was elevated to the vice-presidency in 1973?

Gerald Ford was the Republican minority leader in the House of Representatives for nearly nine years prior to his appointment to the vice-presidency.

Besides both being Presidents, in what other ways were the political careers of Theodore Roosevelt and Franklin D. Roosevelt similar?

Both Roosevelts broke into politics by being elected to the New York legislature. Both served as Assistant Secretary of the Navy (Theodore under McKinley, Franklin under Wilson). Both were elected governor of New York. Both ran for Vice-President— Theodore successfully in 1900, Franklin unsuccessfully in 1920. Both tried to win the presidency for more than two terms. Theodore failed; Franklin went back to the White House for a third term and was elected to a fourth term that was cut short by his death in 1945.

Who was President when the United States first had 50 states?

Dwight D. Eisenhower, who was President when Alaska and Hawaii became states in 1959.

Too much money in the treasury was the most pressing problem faced by what President?

Chester A. Arthur. When he took office in 1881, there was a huge treasury surplus caused mainly by high tariffs and low government expenditures. This created a problem because with each increase in treasury funds, more money was taken out of circulation, causing a deflation of prices. President Arthur urged Congress to lower the tariffs, but the powerful manufacturers had more influence with Congress, and in 1883 tariffs were raised rather than lowered.

In what President's administration did a peacetime Congress first spend a billion dollars?

Benjamin Harrison was President (1889-1893) when the first peacetime Congress appropriated a billion dollars. This quickly disposed of the large treasury surplus that had concerned earlier Presidents. Having too much money in the treasury has not been a problem for any Presidents in the twentieth century.

What President first made the often-quoted statement: "He serves his party best who serves his country best"?

Rutherford B. Hayes.

What President originated such familiar phrases as "my hat is in the ring," "lunatic fringe," and "muckrakers"?

Theodore Roosevelt.

Earl Warren was appointed Chief Justice of the Supreme Court by what President?

By Dwight D. Eisenhower, in 1953. Conservative President Eisenhower was astonished and angered by some of the liberal decisions made by the Court under Warren's leadership.

Who was the first incumbent President to visit Japan and later to attend a conference with 36 other world leaders at Helsinki, Finland?

Gerald Ford.

Who was the first President to visit both the Soviet Union and China while in office?

Richard Nixon.

More federal money was spent on the construction of public works in what Republican's one term as President than had been spent in the preceding 36 years?

In Herbert Hoover's term as President, from 1929 to 1933.

A large-scale highway program, calling for about 41,000 miles of new interstate freeways, was a major accomplishment of what President?

Dwight D. Eisenhower.

What President was called the "father of the American Navy"?

Chester A. Arthur, because in 1882 he persuaded Congress to appropriate funds for the country's first four all-steel ships. At that time the Navy consisted of only a few slow wooden cruisers.

To demonstrate our growing naval strength, what President sent 16 new battleships, called the Great White Fleet, on a world tour in 1907?

Theodore Roosevelt.

Richard Nixon announced his resignation as President on August 8, 1974. What other famous head of state went into exile on an August 8th?

Napoleon Bonaparte on August 8, 1815, sailed for the island of St. Helena to spend the rest of his life there in exile.

How long after Richard Nixon resigned the presidency did President Gerald Ford grant him a "full, free, and absolute pardon" for any crimes he may have committed in connection with the Watergate affair?

On September 8, 1974, one month after Nixon resigned, President Ford pardoned him. The merits of this act are still being debated, but there is no doubt that pardoning Nixon hurt Ford more in the 1976 presidential election than anything else he did while President.

What President most deserves the title of "trust buster"?

Theodore Roosevelt is usually remembered as the great "trust buster," but the title should go instead to William H. Taft. During Taft's four years in the White House he waged twice as many successful antitrust suits as Roosevelt had done in seven years.

What clerk in a small-town store became general-in-chief of all U.S. armies and then President—all within eight years?

Ulysses S. Grant.

What President sent federal troops into Little Rock, Arkansas, to assure compliance with court-ordered school desegregation?

Dwight D. Eisenhower did this in 1957.

What President restricted the Constititutional rights of citizens much more severely than any other President?

President Abraham Lincoln assumed unprecedented power during the Civil War. He allowed many suspected Confederate sympathizers to be jailed without trial and without the right of habeas corpus. In other instances he authorized the use of military courts to try civilians, even in areas where regular courts were operating. Opposition newspapers were denied the use of the mails or seized by troops, and the legislature of Maryland, a border state with many pro-Southerners, was not permitted to convene. Lincoln defended these strong measures because the Union was in peril, and during such an extreme emergency he felt that the survival of the nation was more crucial than the enforcement of Constitutional rights.

What Republican family rivals the famous Adams family because it produced four generations of honest, competent public servants?

The Taft family. Alphonso Taft was Secretary of War in Grant's administration. His son William H. Taft was President and later Chief Justice of the Supreme Court. His grandson Robert Taft and his great-grandson Robert Taft, Jr. were U.S. senators from Ohio.

Republicans were in the White House when the United States ended its involvement in two Asiatic wars that occurred since World War II. Who were these Republican Presidents that ushered in periods of peace?

Dwight D. Eisenhower, who was President at the end of the Korean War in July 1953, and Richard Nixon, who was President when the last American troops were brought home from Vietnam in March 1973.

Why was it ironic that Herbert Hoover made this statement: "Twenty million people are starving—whatever their politics, they shall be fed"?

Herbert Hoover, one of the best examples of a self-made millionaire under the capitalist system, made this remark about the terrible famine in Communist Russia after World War I. Hoover put his humanitarian feelings above politics and directed the sending of large food shipments to the Soviet Union. The Communists later admitted that this food from the United States saved the lives of millions of starving Russians.

What wartime President had been a vigorous antiwar protester when he was a congressman?

Abraham Lincoln, whose one term in Congress occurred during the Mexican War. Congressman Lincoln vehemently opposed the war and offered the "spot resolution," calling for evidence to locate the "spot" where the Mexicans had allegedly started the war by attacking the United States troops.

Land for a canal in Panama was leased and construction of the canal was started in what President's administration?

In Theodore Roosevelt's administration.

What President signed the first civil rights legislation enacted by Congress in 82 years?

In 1957 Dwight D. Eisenhower signed a bill that gave the federal government new powers to protect every citizen's right to vote.

Who was President when the voting age was lowered from 21 to

18 by the 26th Amendment?

Richard Nixon was President when the 26th Amendment went into effect on July 5, 1971.

What President initiated an "Open Skies" proposal that called for the United States and the Soviet Union to permit aerial inspections of each other's territory and the exchange of blueprints of their military installations?

Dwight D. Eisenhower made this proposal at the Geneva, Switzerland, summit meeting in 1955, but it was rejected by the Soviet Union.

What President arranged an agreement that ended school segregation in San Francisco?

In 1907 the San Francisco School Board ordered the segregation of all children of Asiatic ancestry in separate Oriental schools. This greatly offended the Japanese government, so President Theodore Roosevelt offered to help settle the controversy. A "Gentlemen's Agreement" was made, whereby the San Francisco School Board rescinded its segregation order, and the government of Japan promised to end the emigration of Japanese laborers to the United States.

What future President gained national fame as a member of the House Committee on Un-American Activities?

Richard Nixon, who, as a member of this House committee, interrogated Alger Hiss, a former State Department official accused of giving secrets to the Soviet Union.

What President has been called the "father of conservation"?

Theodore Roosevelt. In his administration the government set aside 125 million acres of timberland in national reserves, doubled the number of national parks, sponsored huge irrigation projects to make vast areas of arid land productive, and conserved millions of acres of valuable coal deposits for public use.

Why was it ironic that Chester A. Arthur was President when the act establishing the civil service system was passed?

Earlier in his career Arthur had been the willing tool of a political machine, and due to the spoils system he was appointed collector of the port of New York. But after Arthur became President, he did an about-face and strongly supported the Pendleton Act, which set up a civil service system that largely replaced the spoils system.

About how long did it take Abraham Lincoln to deliver the Gettysburg Address?

The most famous speech in our history was delivered in about two minutes.

What President signed SALT I, the treaty between the United States and the Soviet Union to limit strategic nuclear weapons?

Richard Nixon signed SALT I on May 26, 1972.

During the Boston police strike in 1919, what future President declared, "There is no right to strike against the public safety by anybody, anywhere, any time"?

Massachusetts Governor Calvin Coolidge made this statement, which helped propel him into the vice-presidency and, ultimately, the presidency.

What are the three mistakes in this sentence: "In the Spanish-American War Theodore Roosevelt commanded the cavalry regiment known as the Rough Riders, that charged on horseback up San Juan Hill"?

(1) Lieutenant Colonel Theodore Roosevelt was second in command; Colonel Leonard Wood commanded the regiment. (2) The Rough Riders were a cavalry regiment, but the transport ships carrying them to Cuba were so crowded that all of the soldiers, except the officers, had to leave their horses behind. (3) The charge was made on Kettle Hill, not San Juan Hill.

After the Spanish-American War and the Filipino insurrection against American rule, what future President became civil governor of the Philippines?

William H. Taft was given this difficult assignment in 1901. He helped heal the wounds caused by the bloody insurrection that lasted two years. Taft supervised the building of schools, roads, and hospitals and the development of a stronger economy for the islands. Unlike many colonial governors, Taft gained the respect and affection of the Filipino people.

What future President and Soviet premier engaged in a televised "kitchen debate" over the merits of capitalism?

In 1959 Vice-President Richard Nixon engaged in a heated exchange with Soviet Premier Nikita Krushchev inside the model kitchen of a U.S. exhibit at a Moscow fair.

What Republican President promised he would serve only one term in the White House—and kept his promise?

Rutherford B. Hayes.

Who was the first woman to serve in the Cabinet of a Republican President?

Oveta Culp Hobby, who was appointed the first Secretary of Health, Education, and Welfare by President Eisenhower in 1953.

Who were the only three Republican senators to become President?

Benjamin Harrison and Warren G. Harding, both from Ohio, and Richard Nixon from California.

Six Republican members of the House of Representatives later became Presidents. Who were they?

Abraham Lincoln from Illinois, James A. Garfield, Rutherford B. Hayes, and William McKinley from Ohio, Richard Nixon from California, and Gerald Ford from Michigan.

Six Democratic Secretaries of State later became Presidents. How many Republican Secretaries of State later became Presidents?

None.

Only two Republican Cabinet members became Presidents. Who were they?

William H. Taft served as Secretary of War under Theodore Roosevelt, and Herbert Hoover was Secretary of Commerce in the administrations of Harding and Coolidge. (Ulysses S. Grant was appointed Secretary of War by President Andrew Johnson, but his nomination was not confirmed by the Senate.)

How many men that President Richard Nixon appointed to the Supreme Court were confirmed by the Senate?

Four—Chief Justice Warren Burger and Associate Justices Harry Blackmun, Lewis Powell, and William Rehnquist.

How many men that President Richard Nixon appointed to the Supreme Court were not confirmed by the Senate?

Two—Clement Haynsworth and G. Harrold Carswell.

How many appointments to the Supreme Court did President Gerald Ford make?

One—Associate Justice John Paul Stevens.

Why was Abraham Lincoln's Emancipation Proclamation more important as propaganda than as an order to free the slaves?

Because it freed only the slaves in Confederate territory, and obviously these blacks could not be emancipated unless Union troops physically occupied the areas where they lived. But the Emancipation Proclamation bolstered sagging morale in the North and, perhaps even more important, won sympathy for the Union cause abroad.

Why didn't the Emancipation Proclamation declare that all slaves in America were to be freed immediately?

Because some of the border states that fought on the Union side, such as Missouri and Kentucky, still had slavery, and Lincoln was shrewd enough not to disturb the status of slavery in these states as long as their help was needed to win the war. After the war ended, the 13th Amendment, which freed slaves in every part of the nation, was added to the Constitution.

Was Spiro Agnew the first Vice-President to resign?

No. John C. Calhoun resigned as Andrew Jackson's Vice-President in 1832 in order to serve in the Senate from South Carolina.

What four Republican Vice-Presidents were elevated to the presidency when the President died or resigned?

Chester A. Arthur, Theodore Roosevelt, Calvin Coolidge, and Gerald Ford.

Only one time has the United States had both a President and a Vice-President who were not elected to these offices. Who were they?

Both President Gerald Ford and Vice-President Nelson Rockefeller were not elected to their offices. President Richard Nixon had appointed Gerald Ford to the vice-presidency in 1973 after the resignation of Spiro Agnew. When Nixon himself resigned in 1974, Ford became President and appointed Nelson Rockefeller to be the new Vice-President.

Why was Richard Nixon the first President to appoint a Vice-President?

The 25th Amendment, added to the Constitution in 1967, provides that when the vice-presidency is vacant the President can appoint someone to fill that office, whose nomination then must be confirmed by a majority vote of both houses of Congress. Before 1967 seven Vice-Presidents died in office, but the position remained vacant until after the next election. In fact, while James Madison was President, the Vice-President in his first term, George Clinton, died in office, and so did the Vice-President in his second term, Elbridge Gerry.

What two women did President Ronald Reagan appoint to his Cabinet in 1983?

Elizabeth Hanford Dole, the wife of Senator Robert Dole of Kansas, was appointed Secretary of Transportation. Margaret Heckler, a former congresswoman from Massachusetts, was named Secretary of Health and Human Services.

President Reagan in 1983 signed into law a bipartisan reform bill that was intended to save what major domestic program from possible bankruptcy?

Social Security.

In 1984 President Reagan announced what new goal for America's space program?

The first manned space station that would continuously orbit the earth. The President envisioned the station as an effort to "build on America's pioneer spirit and develop our next frontier."

Did the economy experience any roller-coaster effect after Reagan moved into the White House?

Yes. In 1981 and 1982 the economy suffered a severe recession in which millions of people were thrown out of work and productivity declined sharply, especially in the large automobile and housing industries. But economic conditions improved steadily in 1983, and before the end of the year there were many signs that a full-blown recovery was under way. This recovery continued to escalate in 1984.

Despite vigorous protests in some of the NATO countries, President Reagan was determined to move ahead with the program to deploy Pershing II and cruise missiles in Western Europe, beginning in 1983. Was this mission carried out?

Yes.

The Reagan administration supported with military and economic aid the guerrilla warfare against left-wing rebels in what Central American country?

El Salvador.

At the same time the Reagan administration was helping insurgents who were trying to topple the left-wing government of what other Central American country?

Nicaragua

The greatest military achievement in Reagan's first term involved the liberation of what Caribbean island?

Grenada.

Where did the most serious military setbacks occur during Reagan's first four years in the White House?

In Beirut, Lebanon, where terrorists attacked Americans three times in 1983 and 1984. Their attack in October 1983 killed 241 U.S. servicemen and led to the withdrawal of our peacekeeping forces from trouble-ridden Lebanon.

FIRST LADIES

What First Lady moved her large family, including children, grandchildren, father, niece, and in-laws into the White House in 1889—and then discovered that the place had only one bathroom?

Caroline Scott Harrison, the first Mrs. Benjamin Harrison. She felt that living conditions for the President's family were intolerable and had three separate sets of plans drawn for drastic renovation of the White House. But a stingy Congress rejected all the plans. Mrs. Harrison persisted, however, and finally Congress appropriated $35,000 to refurbish the Executive Mansion. The old building got new paint, wallpaper, flooring, and, most important, more bathrooms.

While she was in the White House, what First Lady learned that her brother had been murdered by his lover?

In 1898 Ida McKinley was shocked by the news that her brother George Saxton had been killed by an unhappy divorcee whom he would not marry. Apparently Saxton was a notorious libertine, and when the murderer was freed by a sympathetic jury, the crowd in the courtroom cheered.

What President's wife was such a plump toddler that her mother hung a sign on her back saying, "Please do not feed this child"?

Fat little Betty Bloomer, who grew up to become slender Betty Ford.

In her youth what Republican First Lady dated a Democrat who later ran against her husband for the presidency?

Before Mary Todd married Abraham Lincoln, she dated Democrat Stephen A. Douglas, who ran against Lincoln in the 1860 presidential election.

What First Lady worked her way through the University of Southern California by taking part-time jobs as a motion-picture extra?

Pat Nixon.

What First Lady served as a volunteer nurse during the Boxer Rebellion?

Lou Hoover. She and bridegroom Herbert Hoover sailed for China on their wedding day in 1899. When the Boxer Rebellion broke out in 1900, the Hoovers were among 200 foreigners besieged in Tientsin. While Mrs. Hoover helped care for the sick and wounded, her husband worked to strengthen fortifications and procure food and drinking water until the month-long siege ended.

What caused Mamie Eisenhower's frequent dizzy spells?

Meniere's disease, a persistent inner-ear disturbance. Rumors mistakenly attributed her dizziness to drinking.

What President's wife was chiefly responsible for bringing the cherry trees to Washington, D.C.?

Helen Taft had seen the beautiful blossoms of cherry trees in the Far East, and she wanted the same kind of trees for the nation's capital. Her wish was granted when the mayor of Tokyo sent 3,000 cherry trees as a gift from Japan to the United States, and Mrs. Taft planted the first one herself in 1912.

The parents of what future President refused to attend his wedding because they strongly opposed slavery, and their son was marrying into a slave-owning family?

Ulysses S. Grant's parents wouldn't attend his wedding in St. Louis because his bride, Julia Dent, belonged to a family of slaveholders.

What First Lady was held up at gunpoint when she was a bank teller?

This happened to Pat Nixon, when she was an 18-year-old

teller at a bank in Artesia, California. With the muzzle of a gun pointed at her, she emptied the cash drawer, and the robber got away with several thousand dollars. Later he was apprehended, and Pat's testimony in court helped convict him.

What First Lady divorced her first husband and rejected her only child?

Florence Harding divorced her indolent, heavy-drinking first husband, Henry DeWolfe. She showed little interest in their son Marshall and let her parents adopt the boy. Even after Florence married Warren G. Harding (five years her junior) and had a home of her own, her son continued to live with his grandparents. Both Henry and Marshall DeWolfe died at age 35; both were regarded by Florence as failures; both were buried in unmarked graves.

What President's wife spent many hours every week weeding the White House gardens and tending the flowers?

Lucy Hayes. She felt that the White House belonged to all Americans and it was her duty to help keep the gardens in good shape.

What type of work did Grace Coolidge do before she was married?

She taught handicapped children at the Clarke Institute for the Deaf in Northampton, Massachusetts.

What First Lady met her husband at a coasting party in which they shared a bobsled?

Helen Taft.

What First Lady had a brother, three half-brothers, and three brothers-in-law in the Confederate army?

Mary Todd Lincoln.

Who was the first President's wife to graduate from college?

Lucy Hayes, who graduated from Ohio Wesleyan University in 1850.

What First Lady's sons kept a four-foot alligator as a pet?

Betty Ford's sons.

What First Lady saved the children's Easter-egg-rolling custom in Washington, D.C.?

Lucy Hayes. Ever since James Madison's presidency, Washington children had enjoyed rolling Easter eggs on the Capitol grounds. But during the Hayes administration the Capitol gardeners claimed that the grass was being ruined by the swarms of children who once a year charged across the lawn. Mrs. Hayes, however, insisted that the egg-rolling custom meant too much to the children to be allowed to die. So she invited Washington children to hold this annual event on the White House lawn instead. This kept the tradition alive for future generations to enjoy.

What First Lady's real first name was Thelma?

Pat Nixon was christened Thelma Catherine Patricia Ryan but was called Pat from the day she was born. Her father, a Nevada silver miner of Irish descent, called his daughter Pat because she was born on the eve of St. Patrick's Day.

What First Lady was a guest at the White House when she was 17 and decided then that someday she wanted to live there?

Helen Taft.

What First Lady was not her husband's first wife, even though they had virtually grown up together?

As children, Edith Carow and Theodore Roosevelt lived near each other, and Edith spent much time in the Roosevelt home because she and Theodore's sister Corinne were close friends. Theodore, Edith, and Corinne like to share books and take long nature walks together. After Theodore went away to Harvard, however, he fell madly in love with a beautiful Boston girl, Alice Lee. They were married in 1880, but four years later Alice died. In 1886 Edith Carow became the second wife of Theodore Roosevelt.

What First Lady met her husband because he was her brother's college roommate?

Julia Grant, whose brother and husband both went to West Point.

What First Lady was so extravagant that she bought 300 pairs of gloves in four months?

Mary Todd Lincoln. She often had wild buying sprees and by the summer of 1864 owed merchants $27,000, mainly for clothes. Mrs. Lincoln had a quirk about wearing gloves nearly all the time, and she tried to force her husband to wear them, too. But Abraham Lincoln disliked the idea and kept stuffing the gloves into his coat pockets until one day, when his pockets were bulging, he found eight pairs hidden away.

The two daughters of what President and First Lady died while they were still young children?

William and Ida McKinley's two daughters. Katherine died when she was three, and baby Ida died in her first year. The McKinleys had no other children.

What President and his wife translated a Latin manuscript written in the 1500s?

Herbert and Lou Hoover translated Agricola's *De Re Metallica*, a Latin treatise on mining that was written in 1556. About 3,000 copies of their translation were privately published and presented to universities, mining institutions, and engineering firms.

What President's wife was known as the "First Lady of Baseball"?

Grace Coolidge, who was an avid fan of the old Washington Senators. She went to games as often as possible and listened to others on the radio.

What First Lady became an expert bowler in the basement alleys at the White House, but once dropped a bowling ball squarely on the President's toes?

Pat Nixon.

What First Lady saw her future husband for the first time when he was standing near an open window, shaving—and wearing a hat?

When Grace Goodhue was watering plants outside the school where she taught, she looked across the street and through a window saw a stranger wearing a hat as he shaved. When she later was introduced to Calvin Coolidge, he told her he had a cowlick that would lie flat on his head only if he pressed it into place with a hat each morning.

How did Helen Taft feel about President Theodore Roosevelt possibly appointing her husband to the Supreme Court?

She opposed it. One evening when President Roosevelt and the Tafts were dining at the White House, Teddy whimsically said he could see something hanging over Taft's head. "At one time it looks like the presidency," he said. "Then again it looks like the chief justiceship."

"Make it the chief justiceship," Taft replied happily.

"Make it the presidency," Mrs. Taft insisted, and she won the argument.

What Republican First Lady married her teacher?

Lucretia Garfield. Her future husband, James Garfield, was one of her teachers at Western Reserve Eclectic Institute in Hiram, Ohio.

What First Lady followed her husband to battlefields and once slipped through enemy lines, barely escaping with her four-year-old son?

Julia Grant.

What First Lady and her husband moved 27 times in 37 years?

Mamie and Dwight D. Eisenhower, whose Army career took them to many parts of the world.

What First Lady's bout with breast cancer helped women throughout the country become more aware of the symptoms of this common form of cancer?

Betty Ford.

What subjects did Pat Nixon teach in high school?

Typing and shorthand.

What First Lady burned her husband's private papers shortly after his death?

Florence Harding. Her motive may have been double-edged to destroy any evidence that might have linked President Harding to government scandals, such as Teapot Dome, and to conceal from the public letters that revealed his extramarital love affairs.

What Republican President's wife had the longest life?

Mary Harrison, the second wife of Benjamin Harrison, who lived to be nearly 90 and survived her husband by 46 years.

In her old age what First Lady was a close friend of Varina Davis, widow of Confederate President Jefferson Davis?

Julia Grant.

What First Lady fainted at her husband's inaugural ball?

Ida McKinley. She had one of her frequent epileptic fainting spells while standing in the receiving line, and her husband quickly and quietly carried her from the ballroom.

How did Mrs. Theodore Roosevelt avoid shaking hands with hundreds of persons at public receptions?

By appearing at the receptions with a large bouquet of flowers in her arms.

What President's wife had a career as a professional dancer and model?

Betty Ford worked several years as a dancer and model, and she studied dance under Martha Graham. When her husband was in the House of Representatives, Mrs. Ford trained the wives of Republican congressmen to model in charity fashion shows.

What was Mamie Eisenhower's real first name?

Mary.

What First Lady kept her son in college during the first part of a war because she feared he might be killed or injured in battle?

Mary Todd Lincoln kept her oldest son, Robert, in college after the Civil War started. Robert finally volunteered, but only after his father got General Grant to find him a safe job at headquarters.

What President's wife served as the national president of the Girl Scouts and often entertained scouts at the White House?

Lou Hoover.

What First Lady was the first president-general of the Daughters of the American Revolution?

Caroline Scott Harrison, the first Mrs. Benjamin Harrison.

Why did Mrs. Grant refuse to have an eye operation?

Julia Grant's eyes were crossed, and she was tempted to have a recently developed operation to correct this condition. Her husband, however, talked her out of the operation because he insisted he liked her the way she was.

What First Lady had a narrow escape in Venezuela?

In 1958 Pat Nixon accompanied her husband, who was then Vice-President, on a goodwill trip to South America. The Nixons were confronted by violent anti-U.S. demonstrators in Caracas, Venezuela. The angry mob stormed their motorcade, shattered car windows, spat upon the Nixons, and were starting to overturn their cars when Secret Service agents and police finally beat them back.

What First Lady's mother was a Broadway stage actress?

Nancy Reagan's mother, who was known professionally as Edith Luckett.

What First Lady's name at birth was Anne Frances Robbins?

This was Nancy Reagan's name. Her father was Kenneth Robbins, a New Jersey car salesman, who left his wife shortly after Nancy was born.

In her theatrical career Anne Francis Robbins was known as Nancy Davis. Why was her name changed?

Ever since she was an infant, she was called Nancy. Her mother's second husband was Dr. Loyal Davis, a prominent Chicago neurosurgeon, who adopted Nancy and gave her his family name.

How did it happen that Nancy Davis knew Barry Goldwater many years before she met her husband?

When she was a child, her family vacationed in Arizona, and Goldwater was a neighbor and close friend.

Where did Nancy Davis go to college?

She attended Smith College in Massachusetts and earned a B.A. degree.

What happened to Nancy Davis's college sweetheart?

When he was running to catch a train to meet Nancy for a date, he slipped on the railroad track and was killed by an on-rushing locomotive.

In what show did Nancy Davis get her first big break on Broadway?

In 1946 she played a small but important role in the musical hit *Lute Song*, which starred Mary Martin and Yul Brynner and ran for about six months on Broadway. She played an Oriental girl in *Lute Song* and had her hair dyed black for the part.

What romantic movie hero did Nancy Davis date when she lived in New York?

Clark Gable.

How did Nancy Davis and Ronald Reagan meet?

Nancy Davis moved to Hollywood to begin her film career in 1949, and a couple of years later she discovered that her name was appearing on lists of Communist sympathizers. This distressed the young actress, who asked director Mervyn LeRoy what could be done about the problem. LeRoy introduced her to Ronald Reagan, who was then president of the Screen Actors Guild and one of the leaders in the movement to rid the film industry of Communists. Reagan looked into the case, discovered that there were four women named Nancy Davis in the movie business, and helped the young actress get her name off the Communist lists.

Why was Reagan on crutches when he and Nancy had their first date?

He had broken his leg in a charity baseball game.

How many movies did Nancy Davis make?

She made 11 movies during a career that lasted seven years, until she retired in 1956 to be a full-time wife and mother.

Which of her films does she think was the best?

Night Into Morning (1951) in which she starred with Ray Milland and John Hodiak.

Did Nancy Reagan ever appear in a movie with her husband?

Yes. The Reagans (who were married in 1952) appeared once on the screen together—as an engaged couple in *Hellcats of the Navy* (1956). This was Mrs. Reagan's last movie role.

Nancy Reagan is the mother of how many of the four Reagan children?

She is the mother of Patti, born in 1952, and Ronald, born in 1958. Reagan and his first wife, Jane Wyman, had one daughter, Maureen, and an adopted son, Michael.

To what social cause does Nancy Reagan devote much time and attention?

The fight against drug and alcohol abuse among the young.

Mrs. Reagan recorded what "first" in the history of First Lady crusades?

In October 1983, she served as co-host of ABC's *Good Morning America* and interviewed authorities on drugs, worried parents, and persons who overcame their addictions. Later Mrs. Reagan narrated the Public Broadcasting Service's program, *The Chemical People*, which also dealt with the drug problem.

CAMPAIGN TRAILS, 1860-1900

"We view with alarm the reckless extravagance which pervades every department of the Federal government." When was the first time that this belief was included in the Republican Party platform?

In 1860—the first election in which the Republican candidate (Abraham Lincoln) won the presidency.

Was Abraham Lincoln favored to win the Republican nomination in 1860?

No, the front-runner was New York Senator William H. Seward. So certain were Seward's supporters of his nomination that they put a cannon on the lawn of his home in Auburn, New York, to be fired as soon as the telegraph wire brought word of victory from the Chicago convention. Seward, however, had numerous enemies in the party because of his radical antislavery stand. Lincoln was one of several favorite-son candidates, but he had an advantage over the others because he had few enemies. Also, the rail splitter from Illinois would run strongly in the Mid-western states, which the Republicans needed to win the election.

Lincoln wired his campaign managers: "I authorize no bargains, and will be bound by none!" Was this order obeyed?

No, Lincoln's lieutenants ignored his instructions. To get their man nominated they engaged in some of the most unscrupulous wheeling-and-dealing ever practiced at a political convention. In return for Indiana's votes they promised Caleb Smith, chairman of that state's delegation, the post of Secretary of the Interior in Lincoln's Cabinet and William Dole the job of Commissioner of Indian Affairs. They bought Pennsylvania's large bloc of votes by dangling in front of Simon Cameron, the Pennsylvania boss, the chance to be the next Secretary of War.

After Lincoln won the nomination, he was horrified to discover the deals his managers had made behind his back. But he felt duty-bound to honor the commitments made for him, so he reluctantly gave the politicians the offices they had been promised. Cameron, however, was such an inefficient, corrupt Secretary of War that Lincoln had to dismiss him from his Cabinet in 1862. He demoted Cameron to what then was considered an insignificant, third-rate position in which he could do no harm—U.S. minister to Russia.

How did "Honest Abe's" campaign managers pack the convention hall with Lincoln supporters?

The night before the convention opened, Lincoln's scheming managers had tickets of admission printed that looked exactly like the legitimate ones. The next morning, while confident Seward enthusiasts marched in a parade through the streets of Chicago, Lincoln supporters used their forged tickets to fill every seat in the convention galleries. After the parade the furious Seward contingent tried in vain to get inside the hall. Meanwhile the delegates on the floor were astonished and impressed by the roaring ovation from the galleries every time Lincoln's name was mentioned. "Honest Abe" must be the people's choice, many delegates surmised. On the third ballot they gave this longshot candidate—whose entire experience in the national government was two years in Congress more than a decade earlier—the Republican nomination for the highest office in the land.

In how many cities and towns did Lincoln give speeches during

the presidential campaign?

None. He remained home in Springfield during the entire campaign (as was the custom of most presidential candidates until the twentieth century). He wrote newspaper articles explaining his views, answered letters, and shook the hands of many visitors who came to Springfield to meet him. (Compared with the almost unbearable exertion of modern candidates, running for President in the horse-and-buggy era was about as taxing as swinging in a hammock.)

On November 6, 1860, Abraham Lincoln was elected the 16th President of the United States. (See pages 127 and 128 for the 1860 election results.)

Did Lincoln's outstanding record during his first term in the White House virtually guarantee his reelection?

No. As the 1864 election approached, the tragic and unpopular Civil War still dragged on, and many Northerners blamed the President for their suffering and frustration. Lincoln was caught in the cross fire between those who accused him of lacking the ability to bring the war to a successful conclusion, and those who felt that he was too stubborn to admit that the war was a failure and should be ended without further bloodshed.

A "dump Lincoln" movement developed among some Republican leaders. They wanted to replace the President with his own Secretary of the Treasury, Salmon P. Chase, as their 1864 nominee. "Mr. Lincoln is already beaten," wrote newspaper editor Horace Greeley. "He cannot be elected. And we must have another ticket to save us from utter overthrow."

Why did the Republican Party change its name for the 1864 election?

During the Civil War the Republican Party tried to broaden its base by appealing to Democrats, as well as Republicans, who supported the Union cause. So in 1864 the GOP was temporarily called the Union Party. Much to the chagrin of some party leaders, it nominated Abraham Lincoln to run for a second term. His running mate on the Union Party ticket was Andrew Johnson of Tennessee, a War Democrat who had stayed loyal to the United States even after his own state seceded.

What famous political phrase did Lincoln invent when he learned he had been nominated for reelection?

Lincoln declared that while the convention delegates had not decided that he was "either the greatest or best man in America. . .they have concluded it is not best to swap horses while crossing the river. . . ."

Why did Lincoln's Democratic opponent refuse to run on his own party's platform?

Union General George B. McClellan was the Democratic nominee in 1864. He was determined to drive from the White House the President who three times had stripped him of his command because Lincoln claimed he was too hesitant on the battlefield. But the disgruntled general repudiated the Democratic platform that called for an immediate peace without victory for either side. "I could not look in the face of my gallant comrades of the army and navy," confessed McClellan, "...and tell them that their labors and the sacrifices of so many of our slain and wounded brethren had been in vain; that we had abandoned that Union for which we have so often periled our lives."

What secret note revealed how Lincoln felt about the election?

On August 23, 1864, Lincoln wrote a brief statement and asked his secretaries to endorse it on the back of the paper—without knowing what they had signed. The note said: "This morning, as for some days past, it seems exceedingly probable that this administration will not be reelected. Then it will be my duty to so cooperate with the President-elect as to save the Union between the election and the inauguration; *as he will have secured his election on such grounds that he cannot possibly save it afterwards.*"

Not until after the election did Lincoln's secretaries learn the contents of this secret statement.

What military events helped Lincoln win at the polls?

In the late summer and fall of 1864 the Northern military forces scored some spectacular triumphs—Atlanta fell to General William T. Sherman, Mobile was blockaded by Admiral David Farragut, and the verdant Shenandoah Valley of Virginia was laid waste by General Philip Sheridan. These victories in the field gave a strong shot in the arm to Lincoln's lagging campaign. Large numbers of Northern voters, now sensing that they would soon win the war, cast their ballots for the incumbent President.

What was meant by the "bayonet vote" in 1864?

Shortly before election day, many Northern soldiers were furloughed home so that they could vote, presumably for Lincoln. (It was said that one Pennsylvania soldier cast 49 ballots, one for himself and the others for the absent members of his company.) Other soldiers were allowed to vote at the front. This so-called "bayonet vote" helped increase Lincoln's winning margin over McClellan. (See page 126 for the 1864 election results.)

What was unique about the winning team of Lincoln and Johnson?

This was the only time in our history when we had a Republican President and a Democratic Vice-President.

What Republican President had voted only once before his own election—and that was for the Democratic ticket in 1856?

Ulysses S. Grant.

Without the support of former slaves, would Grant have won a majority of the popular vote in the 1868 presidential election?

No. Grant won the election by 300,000 votes, and about 500,000 newly enfranchised blacks cast ballots for him. Had the election been restricted to white voters only, Horatio Seymour, the Democratic nominee, would have won more popular votes but probably not more electoral votes than Grant. This election demonstrated how vital the black vote was to Republican presidential candidates in the period following the Civil War. (See pages 126 and 127 for the 1868 election results.)

What incredible series of catastrophes beset Horace Greeley, Grant's opponent in the 1872 presidential election?

Within a single month in 1872 Horace Greeley lost his wife, his election for the presidency, his job as editor of the *New York Tribune*, his sanity, and his life. (See page 125 for the 1872 election results.)

The lights literally went out on the candidate favored to win the Republican presidential nomination in 1876. How did this happen?

When the Republican convention assembled in 1876, House Speaker James G. Blaine was virtually certain to be named the presidential nominee. The evening that his name was placed in nomination a wildly enthusiastic demonstration ensued, with hordes of nearly delirious delegates pouring into the aisles, shouting and singing his praises.

Blaine's managers knew that the momentum for their candidate could give him the nomination on the first ballot, so they pressured the convention officials to begin the balloting that same evening. His opponents, meanwhile, realized that they had no chance to stop the Blaine bandwagon if the voting started immediately. Frantically they offered a resolution to adjourn the night session, but it was obvious that this resolution would be easily defeated by the Blaine delegates.

Then the unexpected happened. All the gas lights in the convention hall suddenly went out. The janitors were unable to turn them back on because the building's main gas pipe had been severed (almost certainly by some of Blaine's enemies). So the meeting had to be adjourned. By the next morning some of the euphoria over Blaine's nomination had faded, and his rivals were able to form a coalition that blocked the front-runner. On the seventh ballot dark-horse candidate Rutherford B. Hayes became the GOP nominee and later our 19th President. (See pages 133–135 for the 1876 election results.)

From 1832 until 1936 Democratic conventions required that presidential candidates must win a two-thirds majority of votes to be nominated. Did Republican conventions ever have the same rule?

No, the Republican conventions always followed the rule that a presidential candidate needed only a simple majority of delegate votes to be nominated. This helps explain why Republican conventions usually have needed less time and fewer roll-calls to select their nominees. Between 1856 and 1936 only 7 Republican conventions required more than one ballot to select the man who headed their ticket, while during the same period 11 Democratic conventions needed more than a single ballot to name their standard-bearer.

What Republican convention set the record for the most ballots cast before a nominee was selected?

The 1880 Republican convention chairman had to call the roll of the states 36 times before any candidate received a majority of delegate votes. (This was still far short of the Democrats' record of 103 ballots–during nine days of voting–that were needed to nominate John W. Davis in 1924.)

Why did the 1880 Republican convention need so many ballots to name a nominee?

When President Rutherford B. Hayes declined to run for re-election in 1880, this left the race for the nomination wide open, and a lengthy three-way deadlock developed. Former President Ulysses S. Grant, trying for an unprecedented third term in the White House, was the early leader, but close at his heels were two formidable contenders. James G. Blaine felt, perhaps correctly, that he had been robbed of the nomination four years earlier and this time the party owed him the chance to head the ticket. The third strong candidate was Treasury Secretary John Sherman, who wanted to be President as much as his soldier brother General William T. Sherman wanted to shun the White House. (It was General Sherman who, when prominently mentioned as a possible presidential candidate in 1884, bluntly declared: "If nominated I will not run; if elected I will not serve." Ever since then whenever a presidential prospect unequivocally declares that he will not run, we say he has made a "Sherman-like" statement.)

As the convention balloting dragged on and on, eventually it became apparent that none of the top three candidates could muster a majority of votes. So in desperation the Republican leaders finally turned to a compromise choice, Ohio Congressman James A. Garfield, who won the nomination on the 36th ballot and the election in November. (See pages 132 and 133 for the 1880 election results.)

Why was it ironic that Garfield won the nomination?

Congressman Garfield was the man who had given the nominating speech for John Sherman and never dreamed that the convention would nominate him instead! In fact, when he got a few votes on the 34th ballot, he firmly protested that he was not a candidate. But the harried convention chairman, anxious

to get somebody nominated, ruled that Garfield's protest was
out of order and should be ignored by the delegates.

Who was the only incumbent Republican President to seek his party's nomination for another term and fail to get it?

Chester A. Arthur, who became President in 1881 following
the death of President Garfield, tried in 1884 to be nominated
to run for a term of his own, but the Republican convention by-
passed President Arthur and nominated instead James G. Blaine.

Why was the 1884 presidential election a contest between public dishonesty and private immorality?

Republican nominee James G. Blaine's public reputation was
soiled because he allegedly had used his powerful influence in
Congress to help a railroad company and received in return the
privilege of selling the company's bonds and pocketing a very
high commission. The *Evening Post* claimed that Blaine "wal-
lowed in spoils like a rhinoceros in an African pool," and a
famous political cartoon depicted him, clad only in underpants,
as the "tattooed man," whose entire body was covered with
ugly terms related to his shady deals.

Blaine's Democratic rival, Grover Cleveland, had a record of
outstanding integrity and complete honesty as mayor of Buffalo
and later governor of New York. But his enemies discovered
that in his younger days Cleveland had had an illicit affair with a
Buffalo woman and could have been the father of her illegitimate
child. Although the woman had several suitors, any of whom
might have been the child's father, Cleveland was the only one
who accepted any responsibility for the pregnancy and made
payments for the child's support.

When the Republicans uncovered this embarrassing story,
they chanted in derision:

"Ma! Ma! Where's my Pa?"

To which the Democrats answered:

"Gone to the White House. Ha! Ha! Ha!"

The election was extremely close, with private immorality
(Cleveland) defeating public dishonesty (Blaine) by a whisker.
(See pages 142 and 143 for the 1884 election results and pages
135–137 for the 1888 and 1892 election results.)

In 1896, how did the Republicans cope with the most spellbinding

orator in the political arena?

For emotional exuberance and the ability to bring a wildly cheering audience to its feet with fever-pitch excitement, there have been few speakers in our history like William Jennings Bryan. His fiery "Cross of Gold" speech ranks as one of the best-known American orations.

When 36-year-old Bryan won the Democratic nomination for the presidency, at first the Republicans were puzzled about how to campaign against the "silver-tongued" orator. William McKinley, the Republican nominee, was a better-than-average speaker, but he was no match for the spellbinding Bryan.

So Mark Hanna and the other Republican leaders decided not to have McKinley compete against Bryan as a stump speaker. While Bryan would be barnstorming in one town after another, McKinley would stay at home in Canton, Ohio, and wage a quiet, dignified "front-porch" campaign.

Bryan was obsessed with the idea that the government should permit the unlimited coinage of silver at a ratio of 16 ounces of silver to 1 ounce of gold. McKinley, a strong supporter of gold as the only currency, was adamantly opposed to what he described as Bryan's "silver lunacy."

The Republican newspapers portrayed Bryan as radical and dangerous. McKinley was depicted as stable and serene. He was a God-fearing family man from a middle-size town in Middle America, who sang in the Methodist choir, belonged to the local service clubs, and called all his neighbors by their first names. Furthermore, he had an aged, pious-looking mother, who gently rocked on the front porch as son William shook the hand of every visitor who came to his home. (Many thousands visited McKinley because the railroad companies that supported his campaign provided excursion round-trips to Canton at cut-rate prices.)

The Republican strategy paid rich dividends. Bryan did the stump speaking, but McKinley gathered the votes that sent him to the White House in 1896 and again in 1900. (See pages 128 and 129 for the 1896 and 1900 election results.)

Who lamented, "Now that damn cowboy is President of the United States"?

Mark Hanna, President McKinley's political manager, said this when Vice-President Theodore Roosevelt became Chief

Executive following the assassination of McKinley in September 1901. Hanna had not wanted Roosevelt to be McKinley's running mate in the 1900 election. Roosevelt himself had preferred to continue as the activist governor of New York, rather than serve as Vice-President, a position he regarded as "useless." But Thomas Platt, the New York boss, joined by Matt Quay, the boss in Pennsylvania, succeeded in "kicking Roosevelt upstairs" to the vice-presidency because they claimed he had been totally unmanageable as governor of the largest state in the Union.

What Republican convention had the first woman delegate?

The GOP convention in 1900 had the first—and only, at that time—woman delegate. (The first Republican convention with a significant number of women delegates was in 1920, the same year in which the 19th Amendment gave women the vote.)

CAMPAIGN TRAILS, 1904-1976

What election-eve blunder by Theodore Roosevelt in 1904 haunted him eight years later?

After completing McKinley's term, President Roosevelt was elected in 1904 to serve four more years in the White House. (See page 125 for the 1904 election results.) On the eve of this election victory, Roosevelt announced that "under no circumstances will I be a candidate for or accept another nomination." This was a foolish, unnecessary commitment by the popular Rough Rider, who was then only 46 years of age. When he changed his mind and chose to run again for the presidency in 1912, Roosevelt was made painfully aware of the unfortunate pledge he had made eight years before.

In 1908 whom did Roosevelt handpick as his successor in the White House?

Secretary of War William H. Taft, who was an easy victor over the three-time Democratic nominee, William Jennings Bryan. (See pages 128 and 129 for the 1908 election results.)

Why did Roosevelt seek the presidency again in 1912?

Roosevelt was greatly disappointed with Taft's performance as President. So the two former friends fought furiously for the

Republican nomination in 1912. When Taft was selected as the GOP standard-bearer, Roosevelt refused to retire to the sidelines. Instead, he became the presidential nominee of the new Progressive ("Bull Moose") Party.

How did an eyeglass case possibly save Roosevelt's life?

While he was campaigning in Milwaukee, Roosevelt was shot by a fanatic. The bullet entered the former President's chest. Miraculously, it was deflected by an eyeglass case and small book that Roosevelt kept in his coat pocket, and the bullet lodged in a rib. The Rough Rider insisted on giving his scheduled speech, even though he was bleeding profusely. The wound proved to be minor, but it ended Roosevelt's speaking tour.

The 1912 campaign split the Republican vote between Roosevelt and Taft and sent the first Democrat to the White House in twenty years—Woodrow Wilson. (See pages 149–151 for the 1912 election results.)

What Vice-President, while running for a second term in 1912, died six days before the election?

James S. Sherman, who was seeking reelection as Taft's Vice-President, died on October 30, 1912. Taft won only two states in the election, and the Republican National Committee designated Nicholas Murray Butler, president of Columbia University, to receive the eight electoral votes that would have gone to Sherman had he lived.

What defeated presidential nominee in 1916 later became Secretary of State and then Chief Justice of the Supreme Court?

Charles E. Hughes had resigned as an associate justice of the Supreme Court to run for President on the GOP ticket in 1916. He lost the close election to Woodrow Wilson.(See pages 143 and 144 for the 1916 election results.) Later Hughes was Secretary of State under Presidents Harding and Coolidge (1921–25). In 1930 he returned to the Supreme Court, this time as Chief Justice, and he served until his retirement in 1941 at the age of 78.

About whom was this famous prediction made: "At about eleven minutes after 2 A.M. in a smoke-filled room the party

leaders will pick him as their presidential nominee"?

This prediction was made about Senator Warren G. Harding of Ohio by his campaign manager, Harry Daugherty. It pertained to the 1920 Republican convention in which the nearly even support for the two front-runners, General Leonard Wood and Illinois Governor Frank Lowden, caused a hopeless deadlock. After eight inconclusive roll calls, it was finally agreed that a dark-horse candidate had to be selected to break the impasse. So, at about two in the morning in a smoke-filled hotel room, the party elders gave their approval to Harding. He won the Republican nomination on the tenth ballot and the election in November.

Daugherty's prediction had indeed come true–but the most amazing thing about this prophecy is that Daugherty had made it in February, four months before the convention met! (See page 124 for the 1920 election results.)

Who was the only Republican to ever defeat Franklin D. Roosevelt at the polls?

Governor Calvin Coolidge of Massachusetts was selected as Harding's running mate in 1920, and his Democratic opponent for the vice-presidency was Franklin D. Roosevelt of New York. The ticket of Harding and Coolidge defeated the ticket of Ohio Governor James M. Cox and Roosevelt by landslide proportions.

What Republican was nominated for the vice-presidency in 1924, but refused to accept the nomination?

After Harding's death in 1923, Coolidge assumed the presidency, and the following year he ran for a full four-year term in the White House. The Republican Party wanted former Illinois Governor Frank Lowden as Coolidge's running mate, but Lowden publicly announced he would not run for the vice-presidency. Nevertheless, the Republican convention nominated him and then called a recess to see if he could be talked into changing his mind. But Lowden still refused second spot on the ticket, so the embarrassed delegates nominated former budget bureau director Charles G. Dawes instead. (See page 126 for the 1924 election results.)

Who said, "I do not choose to run in 1928"?

President Calvin Coolidge handed this terse statement to reporters when they asked if he would be a candidate for reelection in 1928. The Republican convention then selected Herbert Hoover, Secretary of Commerce, as its standard-bearer.

How did campaign issues change drastically between 1928 and 1932, the two years when Hoover ran for the presidency?

In 1928 Hoover was elected partly because he favored continuing Prohibition, a popular stand in rural areas and most of the South. Also, Hoover won votes because his Democratic opponent, New York Governor Alfred E. Smith, was a Catholic, which was a major factor in an era of widespread religious intolerance. But the most important issue was the rosy economic outlook—much of the nation had enjoyed unparalleled prosperity under Republican administrations in the 1920s, and the voters wanted to keep in power the party that had been at the helm during these good times.

Just seven months after Hoover moved into the White House, the stock market crashed and the Great Depression began. By 1932, when Hoover ran for a second term, the economic situation again was the overriding issue—only this time the voters blamed the Republican leadership for their hard times and elected Franklin D. Roosevelt to replace Hoover in the White House. (See pages 124 and 151 for the 1928 and 1932 election results.)

What was probably the only bright note for the Republicans in their dismal 1936 presidential campaign?

The colorful yellow-and-brown sunflower, which was the symbol of the Republican nominee, Governor Alfred M. Landon of Kansas, who carried only two states against FDR (See page 151 for the 1936 election results.)

The Democratic Party chose two surprising longshots as presidential nominees in the 1970s—George McGovern in 1972 and Jimmy Carter in 1976. When is the last time the Republicans nominated a longshot candidate?

This last happened in 1940 when the Republicans named Wendell Willkie of Indiana as their standard-bearer. A Democrat until 1938, Willkie had gained publicity as a defender of private enterprise who opposed Roosevelt's public power projects. But he had never run for office before, and his late conversion to the Republican cause led party leaders to speculate that Willkie had almost no chance to win the presidential nomination. A poll taken in early May 1940, showed he was the choice of only 3 percent of Republican voters.

Then suddenly Willkie's campaign caught fire, stoked partly by enthusiastic youth who were drawn to this "non-politician" by his candor and humility. By the start of the convention Willkie had risen in the polls to the point where he was favored by 29 percent of the Republicans, but on the first three roll calls he trailed two better-known rivals, New York District Attorney Thomas E. Dewey and Ohio Senator Robert A. Taft. But on the fourth ballot Willkie surged into the lead. Two ballots later the man who a few weeks before had been dismissed by party leaders as a rank outsider captured the Republican nomination for the presidency. (See page 152 for the 1940 election results.)

When was the only time that both the Republican presidential and vice-presidential nominees died before their terms of office would have been completed?

Wendell Willkie, who was the defeated presidential nominee in 1940, died October 8, 1944. Senator Charles L. McNary of Oregon, the defeated vice-presidential nominee in 1940, died February 25, 1944. If the Republicans had won the election and both the President and Vice-President died in office, the Secretary of State would have become President. (The line of succession to the presidency was changed by legislation in 1947, so that now the Vice-President is followed by the Speaker of the House and then the President *pro tempore* of the Senate.)

When was the last time that a Republican presidential nominee was not chosen on the convention's first ballot?

In 1948, when Thomas E. Dewey was selected as the presidential nominee on the third ballot. That year there were several strong Republican contenders, including Senator Robert A. Taft of Ohio, former Governor Harold Stassen of Minnesota, Senator Arthur H. Vandenberg of Michigan, and Governor Earl Warren of California.

At the 1948 and 1952 Republican conventions who was the floor manager for his home-state candidate, Harold Stassen?

Warren E. Burger of Minnesota, who is now Chief Justice of the Supreme Court.

Who was the only Republican nominee to lose two successive presidential elections?

Thomas E. Dewey, who lost to Franklin D. Roosevelt in 1944 and to Harry S Truman in 1948. (See pages 152 and 144–147 for the 1944 and 1948 election results.)

What precedent began when Dewey gave his acceptance speech at the 1948 convention?

Dewey was the first Republican presidential nominee to appear at the national convention and deliver his acceptance speech to the delegates.

Was General Eisenhower ever approached to run as a Democratic candidate for the presidency?

Yes. In 1948 many Democratic leaders concluded that President Truman was too unpopular with the voters to be returned to the White House, so several months before the convention some prominent Democrats, including James Roosevelt and Hubert Humphrey, tried to convince General Eisenhower to run for President on the Democratic ticket. The general emphatically refused to consider accepting the nomination, nor would he tell anyone whether he was a Democrat or Republican.

In 1952, when General Eisenhower agreed to run for the presidency on the Republican ticket, did he face any strong opposition for the GOP nomination?

Yes. The Midwestern and Southern wings of the party vigorously supported the candidacy of their favorite conservative leader, Senator Robert A. Taft of Ohio. Taft, then 61, had been the number-one champion of Republicanism since the lean New Deal days. Twice before, in 1940 and 1948, he had sought in vain the GOP nomination, and conservative party "regulars" felt he could not be denied it again.

But the Taft camp had not reckoned with the challenge from a beloved war hero who became the most charismatic figure of the decade. When Dwight D. Eisenhower allowed his name to be entered in the 1952 Republican primary in New Hampshire, this was the beginning of a political legend about a plain-speaking general with a boyish grin who captured the hearts of Americans—and the White House for eight years. Still, Taft's loyal supporters gave Eisenhower a tougher fight for the Republican nomination than did his Democratic rival, Adlai Stevenson, in the elections of 1952 and 1956. On the first roll call of the 1952 Republican convention Taft had 500 votes to Eisenhower's 595. (See page 125 for the 1952 and 1956 election results.)

Why did Richard Nixon give his famous "Checkers" speech?

Shortly after the 1952 Republican convention nominated Senator Richard Nixon of California as Eisenhower's running mate, a sensational story about an alleged Nixon "slush fund" made the newspaper headlines. Nixon was accused of secretly taking $18,000 annually from wealthy businessmen for his personal use, and it was implied that in return for this money the senator might have secured Washington favors for his benefactors.

General Eisenhower was stunned and infuriated by this disclosure. His initial reaction was to drop Nixon from the ticket and have the Republican National Committee name someone else to run for Vice-President. But his political advisors urged Eisenhower to give the California senator a chance to defend himself. The general agreed, with the understanding that the only way Nixon could stay on the ticket was to prove that he was "as clean as a hound's tooth."

Nixon decided to wager his entire political future on one half-hour television broadcast in which he would bare his soul and his financial operations to the American public. In a highly dramatic, tearful manner, Nixon explained that the so-called "slush fund" was used entirely for legitimate political purposes, not for personal living expenses. And he declared that he had never accepted any personal gifts, except for a little cocker spaniel named Checkers that his daughters adored.

At the end of his speech Nixon appealed to his television viewers to wire the Republican National Committee, saying whether they felt he should continue to run for the vice-presidency. Telegrams praising Nixon poured into Republican headquarters by the thousands, and when the young senator flew to meet Eisenhower and hear his decision, the general embraced him and warmly proclaimed, "You're my boy!"

How many Republican Presidents have completed their terms and then, as they left office, turned the keys to the White House over to their Vice-Presidents?

None. In fact, only one Republican President even tried to pass his job on to his Vice-President. That was in 1960 when Vice-President Nixon became the GOP presidential nominee, and President Eisenhower supported his unsuccessful campaign. (Only one Democrat who completed his tenure as President was followed into the White House by his own Vice-President. He was Andrew Jackson, who in 1837 was succeeded in the presidency by Martin Van Buren.)

What was the most unusual feature of the 1960 presidential campaign?

The unprecedented series of four hour-long nationally televised debates between the two major-party nominees, Republican Richard Nixon and Democrat John F. Kennedy. Between 70 and 75 million Americans watched the first debate, and the other three drew audiences between 61 and 65 million. In polls taken after the first debate, television viewers gave Kennedy a slight edge, while radio listeners favored Nixon's performance. This interesting discrepancy may have occurred because the TV audience saw some things that would not have been known by those who heard the debate on the radio— Kennedy appeared more poised, confident, and aggressive, while Nixon looked tired and defensive, and his appearance suffered from the stubble of a beard that was noticeable in the glare of bright television lights.

Regardless of who "won" the debates, they helped Kennedy greatly by defusing the argument that at age 43 he was too young and immature to be President.

Who was the first presidential nominee to campaign in all 50 states?

Richard Nixon pledged that he would visit all 50 states in the

1960 campaign, and he kept this promise. Strategically, this probably was not a wise decision. While Nixon was frantically crisscrossing the country to wave at a few Alaskan ranchers and shake the hand of every person in a New England hamlet, Kennedy was spending his time and concentrating his attention mainly on the heavily populated states that had large blocs of electoral votes. In the election Kennedy carried only 23 states, but he had most of the large ones in his victory column. (See page 141 and 142 for the 1960 election results.)

After what election defeat did Nixon berate reporters with this scathing denunciation: "You won't have Nixon to kick around anymore, because, gentlemen, this is my last press conference"?

Nixon unleashed this bitter tirade at reporters after he lost his race for governor of California in 1962 by a much larger margin than he had lost the presidential election of 1960. This stunning defeat in his home state appeared to end his political career. Yet six years later Nixon made perhaps the most remarkable comeback in American political history by rebounding to win the highest office in the land.

Who won the 1964 Republican primary in New Hampshire, the state with the first primary election?

Henry Cabot Lodge, ambassador to South Vietnam, who was an unannounced, write-in candidate, won with 35.5 percent of the New Hampshire votes to 22.3 percent for Senator Barry Goldwater of Arizona and 21 percent for New York Governor Nelson Rockefeller. When Goldwater, the candidate of the conservative wing of the Republican Party, could not gain even one fourth of New Hampshire's votes, this was regarded as a bad omen for his candidacy.

Did Senator Goldwater win most of the state primaries in 1964?

No. Ambassador Lodge won the primaries in New Jersey and Massachusetts. Governor William Scranton carried his own state of Pennsylvania, and other favorite sons captured the Wisconsin and Ohio primaries. Slates of unpledged delegates defeated the Goldwater delegates in Florida and South Dakota. Governor Rockefeller took West Virginia and was a surprise winner in Oregon. But Senator Goldwater did capture the primaries in Illinois, Texas, Indiana, and Nebraska. The crucial primary turned out to be the final one, where conservative Goldwater won a narrow but important victory in California with 51.6 percent of the Republican votes to Rockefeller's 48.4 percent. Goldwater's total in all of the primaries was only 38.2 percent of the ballots cast. But in 1964 only 16 states held primary elections, and the senator from Arizona won a large share of his convention votes from the other 34 states that selected delegates in caucuses and state conventions.

Who was the first woman to seek the presidency on a major-party ticket?

Senator Margaret Chase Smith of Maine. She was a candidate for the Republican presidential nomination in 1964. At the convention she won 27 votes from delegates from seven states.

Did Goldwater win the Republican presidential nomination by a large margin?

Yes. On the first ballot Goldwater had 883 votes, Scranton had 214, and Rockefeller 114.

About whom was Goldwater speaking when he said, "One of the reasons I chose [him] is that he drives [President] Johnson nuts"?

Goldwater was referring to the man he selected as his vice-presidential running mate, William E. Miller of New York. Although Miller was a congressman and the national chairman of the Republican Party, he was not widely known to the American public.

How were the religious backgrounds of the men on the 1964 Republican ticket unusual?

Barry Goldwater, an Episcopalian, had one Jewish parent, and he was the first Republican presidential nominee with a Jewish background. William E. Miller was the first Catholic to run on a Republican national ticket.

How did a single remark in Goldwater's acceptance speech at the convention hurt him badly at the polls in November?

In his convention acceptance speech Senator Goldwater said, "I would remind you that extremism in the defense of liberty is no vice. And let me remind you also that moderation in the pursuit of justice is no virtue." This sincere, forthright statement was widely condemned by the media, which probably caused many people to regard Goldwater as a dangerous "extremist" who should not be elected President. In November, Democratic President Lyndon B. Johnson won a huge election victory. (See page 152 for the 1964 election results.)

Who was the early leader in the 1968 race for the Republican presidential nomination?

Governor George Romney of Michigan, whose impressive reelection victory in 1966 established him as one of the Republican Party's best vote-getters and the early favorite to win the presidential nomination in 1968. In 1967 Governor Romney toured the country, talking to GOP groups in many states. His speeches, however, reduced his popularity because Romney made some unclear, even contradictory statements about national issues.

What off-hand remark virtually ended Romney's chance for the 1968 presidential nomination?

On September 5, 1967, Governor Romney claimed that he had been "brainwashed" by U.S. authorities when he traveled to Vietnam two years earlier. This incredible remark caused his already deteriorating support to crumble quickly. Fearing a probable loss to Richard Nixon in the New Hampshire primary, Romney withdrew as a candidate for the nomination in February 1968. Nixon won in New Hampshire, thus clearing the first hurdle on his way to becoming the presidential nominee.

Since he had lost the presidential election in 1960 and the race for governor of California in 1962, was it very difficult for Nixon to win the 1968 presidential nomination?

No. Nixon had an advantage because he was considered a moderate Republican who could appeal to the various factions in the party. For several years Nixon had campaigned extensively for fellow Republicans in congressional and state elections, and there were many party members around the country who were in his debt. Also, Nixon had lost the presidential election in 1960 by such a thin margin that it seemed logical to give him another chance. Nixon's campaign for the nomination was helped by the indecision and confusing signals of his chief rival, liberal Nelson Rockefeller, who was an off-and-on again candidate. He declared in March 1968 that he was out of the race, and then the following month he got back into the contest. But except for Massachusetts, Rockefeller made a poor showing in the primary elections.

What role did Ronald Reagan play in the 1968 presidential campaign?

Ronald Reagan, who had been elected governor of California in 1966, emerged as the new champion of the conservative wing of the Republican Party. Early in 1968 he declared that he would be a favorite-son candidate but limit his quest for delegates to California. Later he changed his mind. But Governor Reagan waited until the day the convention opened in Miami to announce he now was a serious candidate for the presidential nomination. This was much too late to start a bandwagon rolling his way. On the first and only ballot at the 1968 convention the votes split this way: Nixon 692, Rockefeller 277, and Reagan 182.

What chief factors helped Nixon win the presidency in 1968?

This was a year of widespread unrest, violence in the streets, and escalating protests against the Vietnam War. Nixon successfully appealed to what he called the "forgotten Americans," whom he described as the "non-shouters, the non-demonstrators, that are not racists or sick, that are not guilty of the crime that plagues the land." But to a great extent, the Democrats were their own worst enemies in 1968. Vice-President Hubert Humphrey, the Democratic nominee, was enormously handicapped by being shackled to President Johnson's unpopular Vietnam policies, and his candidacy was the victim of the savage intraparty struggle between the antiwar and prowar factions. The ugly riots and bloodshed outside the Chicago convention hall left the Democratic cause in shambles, even before the fall election campaign began. Then too, the strong third-party appeal of George Wallace cost Humphrey the votes of many normally Democratic blue-collar workers in the large industrial states in the North and Midwest. Even so, Humphrey ran a much better race than either the polls or the political analysts had predicted, and Nixon barely won the close election. (See pages 131 and 132 for the 1968 election results.)

What city was the site originally selected for the 1972 Republican convention?

San Diego, California, was chosen as the host city for the 1972 convention. But party leaders were not certain that the city could provide sufficient protection against possible demonstrations and supply all of the facilities needed for the convention. Also, the media revealed that the International Telephone and Telegraph Corporation had pledged a large sum of money for the San Diego convention site, which embarrassed the Republican officials. So it was decided to shun San Diego and instead hold the 1972 convention in Miami, the same city where the convention had been held four years before.

At the 1972 Republican convention was there much strife or many surprises?

No. The party managers directed the convention as a ceremonial ritual. President Nixon and Vice-President Spiro Agnew were renominated by a unanimous (except for one) vote, so there were none of the exciting floor fights that erupted in many previous conventions. Every event in the 1972 convention followed a minute-to-minute schedule with clockwork efficiency. The script, for example, permitted precisely five minutes for the delegates to demonstrate after Nixon's name was placed in nomination.

Why did Richard Nixon win a second term in the White House by a landslide?

President Nixon began his reelection campaign from a position of strength. Racial tensions had eased, inflation seemed under control, and the unemployment rate was dropping. Our participation in the Vietnam War had declined sharply, and a cease-fire appeared imminent. President Nixon had made historic trips to both the Soviet Union and China. While some conservatives complained that his Administration was "soft on Communism," other Americans applauded the President's friendly overtures to the Soviet Union and China as steps to reduce the danger of a future atomic war.

The Democrats, on the other hand, were feuding among themselves, as they had done in 1968. The Democratic presidential nominee, Senator George McGovern of South Dakota, was too liberal to win the support of most labor unions or the moderate and conservative segments of the party. Also, the McGovern campaign was damaged by serious blunders (including the replacement of the vice-presidential nominee) that helped Nixon achieve a huge reelection victory in November. (See page 124 for the 1972 election results.)

What was the most solidly Republican state in Nixon's 1972 victory and also in Goldwater's 1964 defeat?

If you guess that it was Vermont or Nebraska or Arizona, you are wrong. It was Mississippi, a state with a fascinating political history. Except for 1872, when it was dominated by a carpetbag Reconstruction government, Mississippi had *never* been in the Republican column until 1964, nearly a century later. Even popular Teddy Roosevelt got only 5.6 percent of the state's vote in 1904. The Republican vote in the 1930s and 1940s was almost nonexistent: 3.5 percent in 1932, 2.8 percent in 1936, 4.2 percent in 1940, 6.4 percent in 1944, and 2.4 percent in 1948, the year that Mississippi supported Southerner J. Strom Thurmond and his States' Rights Party. Dwight D. Eisenhower did poll 40 percent of the vote in 1952, but slipped back to a paltry 25 percent in 1956.

In 1960 Mississippi spurned both Republican Nixon and Democrat Kennedy, giving its electoral votes instead to a segregationist noncandidate, Senator Harry Byrd of Virginia. Then in 1964 Barry Goldwater, the victim of Lyndon B. Johnson's steamroller nearly everywhere else, carried Mississippi with a whopping 87.1 percent of the vote! In 1968 only 13.5 percent of the Mississippi voters cast ballots for Richard Nixon, and instead the state supported the third-party candidacy of a fellow Southerner, George Wallace. But only four years later, in 1972, Nixon got an astounding 78.2 percent of the vote!

Then in 1976, when another Southerner was on the ballot, Mississippi returned to the Democratic fold, giving Jimmy Carter a narrow 49.6 to 47.7 percent victory over Gerald Ford. But in 1980 Republican Reagan won the state by 49.4 to 48.1 percent.

The 1976 campaign for the GOP presidential nomination was a two-man race. Who were the two contenders?

Gerald Ford, an unelected President, and Ronald Reagan, the popular former governor of California.

Why was the 1976 New Hampshire primary a serious blow to Reagan's candidacy, even though he won 48 percent of the vote to Ford's 49 percent?

Reagan's campaign managers had confidently predicted a large victory for their candidate in New Hampshire, the state with the first primary election. At that time Ford had never run in an election outside Michigan, and many political experts thought that his record was too limited to impress New Hampshire Republicans. But when the ballots were counted in the Granite State, Ford eked out a narrow victory, which gave his campaign a tremendous psychological boost because he had beaten the favorite. Nevertheless, the way the media analyzed the results seemed unfair to Reagan. Although the Californian polled 48 percent of the vote, television and newspapers portrayed Reagan's loss (by less than 1,600 votes out of 108,000) as a catastrophic defeat.

Where did Reagan get his first big primary victory in 1976?

President Ford followed his New Hampshire triumph with primary wins in Massachusetts, Vermont, Florida, and Illinois. But then his managers became complacent and canceled a presidential trip to North Carolina and last-minute television ads in that state. Reagan campaigned hard in North Carolina, and on March 23 he defeated Ford there decisively. North Carolina gave Reagan's sagging campaign a shot of adrenalin, and he went on to win primaries in nine other states, in addition to picking up many delegates from states that had caucuses instead of primary elections.

Why did Reagan name a running mate before the Republican convention convened?

Going into the convention Ford held a slender lead in pledged delegates. So, in a last-ditch effort to overtake the President, Reagan announced that if he won the presidential nomination, his choice for second spot on the ticket would be liberal Senator

Richard Schweiker of Pennsylvania. This surprising move was designed to win some liberal delegates from the Ford camp. At the convention Reagan's supporters introduced a resolution to force Ford also to name his potential running mate before the delegates would vote on which presidential candidate would head the ticket.

The Reagan strategy backfired in two ways. First, the convention turned down the resolution to compel Ford to announce his choice for the vice-presidential nomination before the presidential nominee was selected. Secondly, some of Reagan's staunchly conservative backers felt miffed by their candidate's alliance with Schweiker, whose views on many key issues were different from theirs and from Reagan's.

How large was Ford's victory margin over Reagan?

There were 2,259 delegate votes at the 1976 convention, and the winning candidate needed 1,130 votes. Ford got 1,187 votes—only 57 more than necessary. This was the closest race for the GOP presidential nomination since 1920, when Warren G. Harding was selected on the tenth ballot.

About how much money in public funds did Gerald Ford and Jimmy Carter receive to finance their general election campaigns?

Federal funding of presidential elections began in 1976, and the Ford and Carter campaigns each received about $21.8 million.

Why were there no televised presidential debates between 1960 and 1976?

A popular incumbent President running for reelection does not need televised debates to promote either his image or his ideas. He already is widely known to the public, and the media report every action he takes and every policy he proposes. The status of his challenger may be enhanced by facing the President on equal terms before a nationwide audience, and these joint appearances certainly give the challenger additional free publicity. Also, the President runs the risk of making some miscue on television that could cost him votes in the election. For these reasons President Lyndon B. Johnson in 1964 and President Richard Nixon in 1972 turned down invitations to debate their opponents.

The situation in 1968 was different because no incumbent was running for the presidency. Hubert Humphrey was anxious to debate Richard Nixon, but Nixon declined. Since he was favored to win the election, Nixon saw little advantage in debating Humphrey.

Since Gerald Ford was an incumbent President in 1976, why did he want to debate challenger Jimmy Carter?

Unlike President Johnson in 1964 and President Nixon in 1972, President Ford was far behind his opponent in the polls when the fall campaign started. So Ford felt he had nothing to lose—and perhaps much to gain—by debating Carter.

How many debates between Ford and Carter were held?

Three.

Who was judged the winner of the Ford-Carter debates?

Pollsters measured public reaction after each of the three televised debates. They concluded that Ford had a slight edge in the first encounter and Carter probably won the last two. The only serious blunder made by either candidate occurred during the second debate when Ford mistakenly said, "There is no Soviet domination of Eastern Europe."

When was the first televised debate between vice-presidential candidates?

In 1976, when there was a single debate between the Republican nominee, Senator Robert Dole of Kansas, and the Democratic nominee, Senator Walter F. Mondale of Minnesota.

Why did Jimmy Carter defeat Gerald Ford in the 1976 presidential election?

The sordid Watergate affair and President Ford's pardoning Richard Nixon were not easily forgotten, and they hurt the Republican cause in 1976. Many voters, still bitter and angry about the Watergate revelations, wanted to throw out of office the "Washington insiders," and, unfortunately, President Ford was the victim of guilt by association. Democrat Jimmy Carter seemed to be an ideal alternative to the typcial Washington politician—a moralistic farmer from a small town, who had no experience in or connections with the national political arena. Furthermore, Carter promised to cut unemployment, control inflation, phase in a national health insurance system, give pardons to Vietnam War resisters, and make new agreements with the Soviet Union to reduce strategic nuclear arms.

Carter won an overwhelming majority of votes from minority groups, especially blacks. He carried nearly the entire South, most of the industrial Northeast, and enough of the Midwest to give him—but only barely—the electoral votes needed to become the 39th President. (See pages 139 and 140 for the 1976 election results.)

What state lost its record of always voting for the winning presidential candidate when it supported Gerald Ford in 1976?
New Mexico.

What city has hosted the most Republican conventions?
Chicago, which has had 14 Republican conventions, the last one in 1960. Philadelphia is the runner-up with 5 conventions.

PURSUIT OF THE PRESIDENTIAL NOMINATION, 1980

The 1980 Republican ticket brought together the candidate with the most convention delegates, Ronald Reagan, and the candidate with the second most delegates, George Bush. In how many earlier elections did the Republican front-runner become the presidential nominee and the runner-up the vice-presidential nominee?

This never happened before in the history of the Republican Party.

Did the Republican Party have more presidential primary elections in 1980 than in any previous year?

Yes. In 1980 there were 36 Republican primary elections, compared to 29 in 1976, 22 in 1972, and only 17 in 1968.

Where were the seven new 1980 primary elections held?

In Connecticut, Kansas, Louisiana, Mississippi, New Mexico, Puerto Rico, and South Carolina.

What percent of Republican convention delegates were selected in primary elections in 1980?

About 75 percent. (As recently as 1968 only about 40 percent of the convention delegates were selected in primary elections.)

Why has the number of presidential primaries greatly increased since 1968?

To give the Republican voters a larger role in the selection of their presidential nominee. It is more democratic to have the rank-and-file party members choose their standard-bearer than to leave this decision largely to party bosses, which was the practice before there were many primaries.

In the past four presidential elections, when there were many Republican primaries, did the GOP convention nominate the "people's choice"— the candidate with the most votes in the primaries?

Yes. Richard Nixon in 1972, Gerald Ford in 1976, and Ronald Reagan in 1980 and 1984 all had the most votes in the primary elections.

Before 1972 did Republican conventions usually nominate the man who had won the most votes in primary elections?

No. Only 5 of the 15 GOP conventions between 1912 and 1968 gave the nomination to the top vote-getter in primary elections. The other 10 GOP conventions (shown below) chose presidential nominees who had not won the most votes in primaries.

Year	Number of primaries	Winner of most primary votes	Presidential nominee	Nominee % of primary vote
1912	12	Theodore Roosevelt	William Taft	33.9
1916	20	Unpledged delegates	Charles Hughes	4.2
1920	20	Hiram Johnson	Warren Harding	4.5
1932	14	Joseph France	Herbert Hoover	33.3
1936	12	William Borah	Alfred Landon	22.0
1940	13	Thomas Dewey	Wendell Willkie	.7
1944	13	Douglas MacArthur	Thomas Dewey	11.6
1948	12	Earl Warren	Thomas Dewey	11.5
1952	13	Robert Taft	Dwight Eisenhower	27.1
1968	17	Ronald Reagan	Richard Nixon	37.5

Besides Reagan and Bush, what other five Republicans waged major campaigns for the presidential nomination in 1980?

John Anderson (who dropped out of the GOP race in April

to run as an independent), Howard Baker, John Connally, Philip Crane, and Robert Dole.

Who was the first Republican to announce he was a candidate for the presidency in 1980?

Congressman Philip Crane of Illinois, who entered the race on August 2, 1978, more than two years before the election.

What other Illinois congressman ran in the presidential sweepstakes?

John Anderson of Rockford, Illinois. In Congress he represented the district that includes Freeport, site of the most important Lincoln-Douglas debate, and Galena, the hometown of Ulysses S. Grant.

A third major GOP candidate was born and grew up in Illinois. Who was he?

Ronald Reagan, who was born in the small town of Tampico and spent most of his youth in Dixon, another small Illinois town.

What presidential contender became a national figure when he was seen on television as the ranking Republican on the Senate Watergate Committee?

Senator Howard Baker of Tennessee.

What GOP candidate was almost killed at the same time President John F. Kennedy was assassinated in 1963?

John Connally, who was then the Democratic governor of Texas and rode in the same car with Kennedy when the President was assassinated in Dallas. Connally also was shot and seriously wounded in this tragic incident.

What candidate was twice elected GOP governor of a state that has three Democrats for every two Republicans?

Ronald Reagan, who was elected governor of California in 1966, defeating the popular Democratic incumbent, Edmund G. "Pat" Brown, by an astounding plurality of nearly 1 million votes. Four years later Governor Reagan was reelected by more than 500,000 votes.

Candidate John Anderson was a Republican congressman for 20 years. During his early terms in the House was he liberal or conservative?

From 1961 to 1968 Anderson was a staunch conservative. He opposed such liberal measures as Medicare, federal aid to education, and government-sponsored urban planning. Three times he sponsored a constitutional amendment that would have declared that the United States is a Christian nation. During most of the 1960s the Americans for Conservative Action (ACA) pointed with pride to Anderson's very conservative voting record.

When did Anderson begin to change his political philosophy and start promoting liberal causes?

In April 1968, Anderson threw his support behind a liberal open-housing bill that eventually passed, partly because he persuaded some of his reluctant Republican colleagues to vote for it. After that time the Illinois congressman began moving farther and farther away from the conservative causes he had previously championed.

What were Anderson's liberal views when he became a candidate for the 1980 Republican presidential nomination?

He opposed a constitutional amendment to prohibit abortions and another amendment that would end school busing to achieve racial integration. He spoke out against the controversial B-1 bomber, the neutron bomb, and a huge buildup of our military forces. He favored the Equal Rights Amendment, a bill for the federal government to finance congressional election campaigns, the Panama Canal treaties, and the ratification of SALT II.

Since Anderson took a liberal position on so many issues, what chance did he have to capture the 1980 nomination of the conservative party?

Anderson had no credible chance of winning the GOP nomination, and this is why the media gave him scant attention when he entered the race. However, he surmised that since his six rivals all were much more conservative, he could capture the support of Republican liberals while his contenders divided the votes of conservatives. But in 1980, except in the Northeast and a few Midwestern states, the liberal wing of the GOP was much smaller than the conservative and moderate groups.

How could candidate George Bush claim both Texas and Connecticut as home states?

Bush grew up in Connecticut and graduated from Yale University in New. Haven. Following college, he moved to Texas, where he entered the oil business and made his home in Houston.

What candidate for the GOP nomination had served a Democratic President as Secretary of the Navy and a Republican President as Secretary of the Treasury?

John Connally, who was President Kennedy's Secretary of the Navy in 1961 and President Nixon's Secretary of the Treasury in 1971-72.

When did Connally leave the Democratic Party to become a Republican?

Connally joined the Republican Party in 1973, at a time when the party was reeling from the effects of Watergate. He explained that he switched parties because he felt that the Democrats had moved too far to the left.

What candidate in the presidential sweepstakes was so severely wounded in World War II that he had to spend three years in hospitals and never regained much use of his right arm?

Robert Dole.

What was Ronald Reagan's "11th commandment"?

"Thou shalt not speak ill of a fellow Republican."

What GOP candidate sponsored a bill in Congress to protect the confidential sources of newspaper reporters?

Philip Crane.

Two of the presidential aspirants previously had served as the national chairman of the Republican Party. Who were they?

Robert Dole was the GOP national chairman from 1971 to 1973, and George Bush held the same position during the troubled Watergate period of 1973-74.

Between the election years of 1976 and 1980, how did Ronald Reagan remain in the political limelight?

He had many speaking engagements throughout the country, wrote a syndicated newspaper column, and broadcast radio commentaries that were carried by about 200 stations.

How did the candidates in the primary elections qualify for public financing?

They had to raise $5,000 in 20 or more states from individuals whose contributions could not exceed $250. This made them eligible to receive about $7 million apiece in matching federal funds.

How much money can an individual or a political action committee give to a presidential candidate's campaign?

The Federal Election Campaign Act of 1974 (which resulted from the Watergate affair) limits individual donations to $1,000 and contributions from political action committees to $5,000.

Which one of the seven Republican presidential candidates refused to take any matching government funds to help finance his primary campaign?

John Connally rejected public funds because accepting them would have forced him, by law, to limit the amount of money he could spend in his campaign. Connally received many contributions, and he raised a large campaign fund without taking any money from the government.

Was Connally still bound by the law limiting the size of contributions a candidate may accept from an individual or a political action committee?

Yes.

Connally spent about $11 million trying to win the GOP nomination. How many convention delegates did he get?

One—Ada Mills of Arkansas.

What Republican won the first state caucuses in the 1980 race for the presidential nomination?

George Bush won a stunning upset victory over heavily favored Ronald Reagan in the Iowa caucuses on January 21.

Remembering that Jimmy Carter's first step up the ladder to the Democratic nomination in 1976 was his surprising triumph in the Iowa caucuses, Bush blitzed that state with speeches, handshakes, and media ads. He began campaigning in Iowa in February 1979, and by the end of November he had made more than 20 trips to the state and had a strong organization of volunteers working for him at the grass-roots level.

Why did Ronald Reagan do poorly in the Iowa caucuses?

Reagan made only a few appearances in the state and declined to join the other GOP candidates in an Iowa debate. Many Iowa Republicans felt that Reagan either had snubbed them or taken their votes for granted. After Reagan later won the nomination, he returned to Iowa and confided to a crowd of 3,000 that "much of the success of my campaign this spring has been due to the results of the Iowa caucuses. You reminded me that no man can stay above the battle if he expects to win the war. You also reminded me that the voters, regardless of the state or the party, expect candidates to come before them and lay out their beliefs and ask for their support."

What happened to George Bush's campaign after he won in Iowa?

Bush temporarily forged ahead of Reagan in the polls, and he boasted that he now had momentum ("big mo") going for him. But actually Bush was not prepared to cope with his new, unexpected role of front-runner. His campaign became overly cautious, and he failed to clarify how he differed with Reagan on some major issues.

Often one key incident marks the turning point in a candidate's campaign. What incident signaled Ronald Reagan's eventual triumph?

A two-man debate between the leading contenders, Bush and Reagan, was scheduled to take place a few days before the nation's first primary election in New Hampshire. The other Republican candidates complained that it was unfair to leave them out of this Nashua, New Hampshire, debate, which was sponsored by a local newspaper. But the newspaper refused to alter its format for a confrontation between just the two front-runners.

Shortly before the debate began, Reagan announced he wanted to open it to all the Republican rivals, and he offered to pay its costs. This was perhaps the most rewarding decision Reagan made during the entire primary campaign. When the debate started, Reagan dramatically grabbed the microphone and demanded that all of his fellow Republicans be heard. People throughout the country were impressed by Reagan's generosity and sense of fair play.

This seemingly innocuous episode in a small town inside a small state marked the beginning of Reagan's steady climb to the goal he was seeking.

When did Reagan regain his lead in the race for the presidential nomination?

In the New Hampshire primary on February 26 Reagan defeated Bush and his other Republican opponents by a comfortable margin. From then until the convention in July, Reagan was at the head of the pack, and most of the subsequent primaries and caucuses widened his lead over his rivals.

Did the election returns in Iowa and New Hampshire have much effect on later primaries and caucuses?

Yes. Out of a total of 1,994 delegates at the Republican convention, only 37 came from Iowa and 22 from New Hampshire. Yet the election results in these two states had an enormously disproportionate impact on the ultimate outcome of the race for the presidential nomination. This ludicrous situation, which might be likened to a one-inch tail wagging a gigantic dinosaur, can be attributed almost entirely to the massive election coverage by the media in Iowa and New Hampshire. Only a tiny fraction of the millions of Republicans across the length and breadth of America indicated their choices in the ballot boxes of these two states. But the media, speaking with a self-appointed authority rivaling that of divine-right monarchs, drew sweeping inferences from the small vote totals, inferences that undoubtedly influenced many voters in later primaries and caucuses.

How many Republican primaries did John Anderson win?

None.

Why then was so much attention focused on Anderson early in the primary season?

Because in primaries on the same day, March 4, Anderson ran a close second to Bush in Massachusetts and a close second to Reagan in Vermont. Also, in two televised debates featuring all the GOP candidates, the Illinois congressman articulated his ideas fluently and forcefully, and he stressed that the election should focus on issues rather than personalities.

When did it become evident that Anderson could not win the Republican nomination?

Anderson was favored to win the GOP primary in Illinois on March 18, partly because this was his home state, and partly because Illinois is one of the few states that permits voters to cross over and cast ballots for a candidate of another political party. Anderson strenuously courted Illinois Democrats and independents to vote for him. But when the ballots were counted, Reagan captured Illinois and Anderson finished a dismal 11 percentage points behind the leader.

Then, on April 1, Anderson's last hope to become the Republican nominee was dashed. In liberal Wisconsin, a state that also allows voter crossovers and where thousands of enthusiastic college-age youth were working the precincts for Anderson, he again was defeated at the polls by front-runner Reagan.

How many primary elections did George Bush win?

Bush won six primary elections. He won in the large industrial states of Pennsylvania, Michigan, and Massachusetts, as well as in Connecticut, Puerto Rico, and the District of Columbia. Also, in Texas Bush captured 47 percent of the vote to Reagan's 51 percent.

Besides Reagan and Bush, did any other Republican candidates win primary elections or caucuses?

No.

When did Bush drop out of the race for the White House?

On May 26 he congratulated Reagan on securing enough votes to win the nomination and released his more than 200 delegates to vote for the Californian on the first ballot.

Which city hosted the Republican convention in 1980?

Detroit, Michigan, hosted its first Republican convention in 1980.

What were the two most controversial issues included in the 1980 Republican Party platform?

One was the plank favoring a constitutional amendment to prohibit all abortions. The other was the plank opposing the Equal Rights Amendment.

Reagan ended his acceptance speech with a long quotation from an address by what President?

Ironically, Reagan quoted from Franklin D. Roosevelt's acceptance speech at the 1932 Democratic convention, in which FDR pledged a government of austerity and fiscal responsibility.

What was the most dramatic event at the 1980 Republican convention?

Ronald Reagan tried to convince former President Gerald Ford to be his running mate. Many convention delegates thought that the combination of Reagan and Ford would be a "dream ticket" because polls showed that Ford was one of the most popular political figures in either party. But there was no historical precedent for a former President's returning to Washington as a Vice-President. The media speculated that Reagan and Ford, if elected, would be almost co-Presidents. But the "dream ticket" never materialized. After Ford declined the vice-presidential nomination, Reagan asked George Bush, his second choice, to share the Republican ticket with him.

Did most American families with TV sets watch the Republican convention?

No. It was estimated that during all four nights of the convention more than half of the television sets were tuned to some other program. Yet the three major networks spent a huge sum of money—about $22 million—to bring this political extravaganza to viewers during prime time. Some television executives speculated that perhaps they should schedule only convention highlights and end the tradition of gavel-to-gavel coverage, which started in 1952 with the first Eisenhower-Stevenson election.

BATTLE FOR
THE WHITE HOUSE, 1980

The Democrats started the 1980 presidential campaign with the advantage of having an incumbent in the White House. Did they also benefit from having a President whom most Americans thought was doing a good job?

No. When pollsters asked the American people in 1980 how they evaluated Jimmy Carter's performance as President, he received lower marks than those of any President since this question was first asked by pollsters in President Truman's administration. The majority of Americans perceived Carter as a weak leader whose domestic and foreign policies were inconsistent and generally unsuccessful.

How did the 1980 national conventions affect the public's perception of the major candidates?

Ronald Reagan led Jimmy Carter by a 37-32 percent margin in the mid-June Gallup Poll, but after the GOP convention in July, Reagan's lead surged to 45-31 percent. Following the Democratic convention in August, Carter bounded back and trailed Reagan by a single point, 39-38 percent. Independent candidate John Anderson's support held steady at 14 percent after both conventions.

How much money did Reagan and Carter receive from the federal government to finance their fall campaign?

They each received about $29.4 million of federal funds for the general election campaign.

Why didn't John Anderson receive the same amount of government money as the two major-party candidates?

The Federal Election Campaign Act of 1974 provided financing to only the Democratic and Republican presidential nominees. But in 1980 when Anderson emerged as a strong contender, the Federal Election Commission decided that he would qualify for some federal funds retroactively, providing he won at least 5 percent of the popular vote in November. But since Anderson did not receive any government money until after the election, his campaign was badly handicapped by its limited financial resources.

Since the government provided funds, were the presidential campaigns limited to federal financing?

No. The Supreme Court ruled that independent groups could raise and spend money for a presidential election, as long as there was no direct collaboration between these private groups and the candidate or his advisers. This court ruling triggered the growth of many political-action committees (PAC's). Some of the larger PAC's, such as the National Conservative Political Action Committee, spent millions of dollars trying to defeat President Carter and liberal candidates for Congress.

What was unusual about the Veterans of Foreign Wars' endorsement of Reagan?

This was the first time in its 81-year history that the Veterans of Foreign Wars, numbering about 2.5 million members, endorsed a presidential candidate.

Did former President Gerald Ford campaign strongly for the Republican ticket in 1980?

Yes. Between Labor Day and Election Day on November 4, Ford campaigned 53 of the 64 days, covering 30 states and about 60,000 miles. No other former GOP President ever traveled so far or made so many public appearances in behalf of other Republican candidates.

Why did Ford attack the Carter administration on economic issues?

Ford claimed that Carter had not kept his promises to lower inflation, reduce unemployment, and bring interest rates down. Ford said that when he left office inflation had been 4.8 percent, but under Carter's presidency it had risen to nearly 13 percent. "Unemployment in my home state of Michigan in the auto industry," Ford asserted, "is over 15 percent, almost as bad as it was during the Great Depression." And interest rates had soared to record heights. The former President concluded that Carter "was handed the economy on a silver platter, and he blew it."

Why did Ford attack the Carter administration on defense measures?

Because of Carter's weak defense policies, Ford declared, "Our allies no longer trust us, our adversaries no longer respect us." A major cause of this problem, according to Ford, was Carter's cuts in defense spending, including delay in building the MX missile system, cancellation of the B-1 bomber, and reduction in the Navy shipbuilding program.

Why did Ronald Reagan contend that increased defense spending offered the best hope for preserving peace with the Soviet Union?

The Republican nominee claimed that if the United States spent enough on defense to achieve a "margin of safety" in strategic weapons, the Soviet Union would not dare to challenge it militarily. On the other hand, the failure of our country to strengthen its defense capacities was a serious threat to peace, Reagan said, because it encourages Soviet expansion and "could back us into war."

Why then did Reagan oppose the military draft registration that President Carter had ordered?

The GOP candidate said that this nation should put its faith in an all-volunteer force that "can and will provide the military manpower necessary for the margin of safety our nation needs in the years to come." He added that serving in the armed forces can be made more attractive by offering volunteers a higher pay scale.

How did Reagan feel about SALT II?

Reagan said he would scrap SALT II, which he described as "fatally flawed," because in his opinion it gave more advantages to the Soviet Union than to the United States. Instead, Reagan called for new negotiations with Moscow toward a weapons agreement more favorable to the United States.

What did Reagan blame for the high inflation rate?

"There is only one cause for inflation," Reagan declared. "Government causes it; therefore, government can make it go away."

What was Reagan's dramatic proposal for cutting income taxes?

Reagan supported the Kemp-Roth plan to slash personal income taxes by 30 percent, phased in at 10 percent a year over 1981, 1982, and 1983. He also backed federal indexing of income tax rates for inflation, so that cost-of-living pay raises "do not continually push workers into higher tax brackets." Reagan claimed that excessively high income tax rates were one of the most significant factors contributing to the nation's economic problems.

Did Reagan think he could balance the federal budget?

Yes, in the 1980 campaign Reagan said he believed he could balance the budget by his third year in the White House.

How did Reagan answer critics who asked how he could increase defense spending sharply, cut income taxes by 30 percent, and still balance the budget?

The chief means of balancing the budget, Reagan asserted, was holding down government spending. He claimed that the federal government wastes billions of tax dollars every year, and if elected President, one of his top priorities would be to end this government waste. Also, Reagan insisted that government tax revenues should be sufficient for all essential expenditures because of greater business productivity caused by (1) lowered individual income taxes, (2) corporate tax cuts in the form of faster depreciation on new tools and equipment, and (3) the ending of several thousand regulations that have caused [industrial] problems.

Reagan was once said to favor a voluntary Social Security system. Did he advocate this during the 1980 presidential campaign?

No. Reagan denied that he wanted to make Social Security voluntary and added, "What I really want to do is put it on a sound basis so that the people dependent on it will know they're going to get their checks. We would be foolish if we didn't pay attention to the fact that Social Security is actuarially out of balance by trillions of dollars." Reagan also described as unfair the regulations that restrict the income that Social Security beneficiaries may earn.

What did Reagan recommend to help solve our energy problem?

The GOP candidate declared that the United States still has large amounts of untapped oil and natural gas, but that government regulations, price fixing, and tax policies have stifled the incentive of American companies to explore and produce these new sources of energy. Reagan felt that if this government interference were lifted, the energy problem could be greatly alleviated.

What did Reagan mean by the "family-suffering index"?

This was a new indicator of President Carter's economic record that the Republican nominee unveiled during the fall campaign. Reagan said that the index—consisting of inflated prices, unemployment figures, and mortgage interest rates—had risen from 24.2 percent to 77 percent since Carter entered the White House.

Why didn't Carter participate in the first presidential debate?

He refused to take part in a three-way debate with Ronald Reagan and John Anderson until after he had faced Reagan alone in a "one-on-one" debate. So when the League of Women Voters asked all three candidates to appear in the first debate, Carter declined the invitation. He claimed it was not fair to ask one Democrat to face two Republicans. But the strategy behind this decision was to prevent Anderson from enhancing his status as a viable candidate, since the Democrats feared that Anderson would take more votes away from Carter than from Reagan.

Was Reagan or Anderson helped the most by their presidential debate?

Reagan apparently was helped the most by the debate on September 21 because after his TV encounter with Anderson his position in the polls began rising again. Immediately after the debate, Anderson's standing in the polls was unchanged, but in October it began to decline sharply.

In the fall campaign did Reagan direct his appeal for votes primarily to those conservative groups that generally support Republican candidates?

No. Reagan's managers knew that their man already had the unswerving allegiance of traditional conservatives. But they also knew that the Republican Party was only the *third* largest political group in our country. There were many more Democrats and also many more independents than there were Republicans. So in order for Reagan to win, he had to attract millions of voters who were not Republicans and usually did not vote for the GOP ticket.

In what normally Democratic strongholds did Reagan campaign vigorously?

He carried his message into the heartland of industrial America, from the automobile assembly lines in Detroit to the steel plants in Ohio, the coal mines in Pennsylvania, and the garment factories in New York City. Reagan waged a more intensive effort to win blue-collar support than any other GOP presidential candidate in this century.

The Republican standard-bearer also campaigned strongly below the Mason-Dixon line and refused to concede that the South, which Carter swept in 1976, would again support the peanut farmer from Georgia.

What issues did Reagan stress when he courted the blue-collar vote?

The pocketbook issues—spiraling inflation and growing unemployment. He also emphasized his concern about our weakening military posture and declining role in world affairs. And

Reagan impressed many workers with his plea for stronger family values and his stand against abortion.

Did any large unions endorse the GOP nominee?

Yes, both the huge Teamsters and National Maritime unions supported Reagan.

Did Reagan concede the minorities' vote to Carter?

No. Even though Carter in 1976 won 75 percent of the Jewish vote, 80 percent of the Hispanic vote, and nearly 90 percent of the black vote, Reagan tried hard to increase the GOP's share of the minority vote. A few prominent minority figures backed the Republican nominee, including the Reverend Ralph Abernathy, a former head of the Southern Christian Leadership Conference and close associate of the late Martin Luther King, Jr.

What former leader of the "doves" in the Vietnam War supported Reagan?

Eugene McCarthy, the former senator from Minnesota, who was an ardent antiwar presidential candidate in 1968 and an independent candidate in 1976.

Why didn't John Anderson appear in the second and final presidential debate?

The League of Women Voters decided that the participants in its presidential debates would include only those candidates whose standings in the major polls showed they were the choice of at least 15 percent of the voters. Anderson cleared this hurdle for the first debate, but by mid-October when the invitations were issued for the second debate, his support, according to most of the polls, had dropped below the 15 percent minimum figure.

How close was the presidential race at the time of the Reagan-Carter debate?

By late October the major polls indicated that the two candidates were running "neck-and-neck," and some gave Carter a slight lead. It appeared that Carter was gaining support, especially among women voters, by claiming that Reagan favored a dangerous arms race with the Soviet Union and was weak on the issue of preserving peace.

Who was the "winner" in the single debate between the two major-party candidates?

This crucial television confrontation between President Carter and challenger Reagan before over 100 million Americans—exactly one week before the election—was called a draw by some debate experts, but polls soon showed that the majority of TV viewers were more favorably impressed by Reagan's performance.

How did Reagan "win" the debate in the eyes of the American public?

First and foremost, Reagan effectively defused the war-and-peace issue that had concerned many voters. "I'm here to tell you," he affirmed, "that I believe with all my heart that our first priority must be world peace, and that use of force is always and only a last resort." The GOP nominee also assailed the Carter economic record, reminding the viewers of the high level of inflation, taxation, and unemployment.

Another, more subtle advantage for Reagan was the image he conveyed to the huge television audience. He was seen as a man with friendly warmth and homespun humility who had a positive, hopeful message for Americans and the determination to put his promises into practice. Carter, on the other hand, appeared taut, somber, and somewhat strident and scolding. But the President was matched against a master TV performer—in fact, it often has been said that former actor Reagan uses this medium more effectively than any other politician since the birth of television.

How did the issue of the American hostages held in Iran influence the election?

Republican leaders were constantly worried about some diplomatic "October surprise" that the President might provide, and they conceded that if the hostages came home before the election this might swing most undecided voters to Carter. The Sunday before the election the Iranian Majlis (parliament) finally voted to free the American captives, providing the United States would comply with four demands.

But this apparent break in the lengthy impasse with Iran failed to improve Carter's chances for reelection. Instead, it seemed to remind voters that Election Day would occur exactly one year after the hostages had been captured, and during that long year of waiting and praying for their safe return, the President was unable to secure their release from a small, relatively powerless country. So to many voters the hostage issue was seen as an example of Carter's inability to assert himself as a strong and successful leader.

Did the fundamentalist religious groups affect the outcome of the election?

Yes. In 1976 many Protestant fundamentalists supported the "born-again" Baptist, Jimmy Carter. But in 1980 large numbers of them voted Republican because they preferred the GOP positions on such issues as abortion, the Equal Rights Amendment, school prayers and busing, national defense, and government spending. Moreover, religious-activist groups like the Moral Majority registered perhaps as many as 4 million new voters to cast their ballots for Reagan and other GOP candidates.

What were the pollsters predicting on election eve?

Most of them felt the election was "too close to call." *Newsweek* and *Time* surveys showed Carter slightly ahead in the popular vote but substantially behind in the electoral count. CBS News/*New York Times* called the popular vote 44- 43 percent for Reagan, and the final Gallup Poll gave Reagan a 47- 44 percent edge. The only poll to suggest a big Republican victory was the ABC News/Harris Survey, but its 45-40 percent forecast was much smaller than the size of Reagan's triumph on Election Day.

Why did the polls fail to detect the Reagan landslide?

Until the last few days of the campaign there were unusually large numbers of undecided voters and people who leaned slightly toward Carter. Many of them made up their minds to vote Republican shortly before the election. The pollsters did recognize that the momentum swung sharply to Reagan following the debate one week before the election. But they did not accurately assess the size of the dramatic shift in voters' sentiments, partly because it continued to grow steadily during the weekend before the election. In defense of the pollsters it should be pointed out that every other presidential election in the past 40 years that appeared to be a "neck-and-neck" race in late October stayed close on Election Day.

How large was Reagan's landslide victory?

The Republican nominee won all but six states and the District of Columbia. His winning margins in both the popular and electoral votes were huge.

	Popular Vote	%	Electoral Votes	%
Ronald Reagan	43,904,153	50.7	489	91
Jimmy Carter	35,483,883	41.0	49	9
John Anderson	5,720,060	6.6	0	0
Other candidates	1,407,125	1.7	0	0

Who was the last Democratic President before Carter to lose an election for a second term?

Grover Cleveland, who lost his bid for reelection in 1888.

Before the election Democratic chieftains claimed that if their nominee lost it would be due to Anderson's taking votes that would have gone to Carter in a two-way race. Did this happen?

Anderson's vote was larger than Reagan's margin of victory in 14 states with a combined total of 158 electoral votes. But even if Carter had won all 14 states, his electoral count would have been only 207, which is 63 electoral votes short of the number needed to win the election. And when pollsters asked Anderson voters at the precincts whom they would have supported in a two-way race, nearly half of them said Reagan. Also, the Anderson factor cuts both ways. In four of the six states Carter carried, his margin of victory was smaller than the combined Reagan-Anderson vote.

What happened in this election to Carter's once solid base of support, the South?

Southerners overwhelmingly rejected their first native son from the Deep South to occupy the White House since Zachary Taylor. Whereas Carter had taken all the states of the Old Confederacy except Virginia in 1976, he lost all of them except his home state of Georgia in 1980.

What state provided the Republicans' largest winning margin?

Utah, where over 72 percent of the voters cast their ballots for Reagan and for the GOP incumbent, Jake Garn, in the Senate race. But in spite of these lopsided Republican wins, Democratic Governor Scott Matheson was reelected.

In which states did Reagan trounce Carter by more than a two-to-one margin?

In these nine states: Alaska, Arizona, Idaho, Nebraska, Nevada, New Hampshire, North Dakota, Utah, and Wyoming.

What is the only state that has been won by Republicans in every presidential election since 1860, except when Goldwater ran in 1964?

Vermont.

What is the only state Reagan carried which no other GOP presidential nominee had ever won, except Nixon in 1972?

Arkansas.

What is the only state that has gone Republican in every presidential election since 1952?

Arizona, which gave Reagan 61 percent of its vote. Arizona also had the distinction of being the state with the best voter turnout in 1980—more than 80 percent of its registered voters went to the polls.

What state that had not gone Republican since Eisenhower's reelection in 1956 provided Reagan his narrowest victory margin?

Massachusetts, where less than 4,000 votes determined the winner. It almost certainly would have stayed Democratic if Anderson had not been in the race.

	Reagan	Carter	Anderson
Massachusetts	1,057,631	1,053,802	382,539

What voter groups gave Reagan his impressive triumph at the polls?

Reagan drew his electoral strength from a wide cross section of Americans in every region of the country. He was a big winner among men voters, whites, farmers, and Protestants. He carried the normally Democratic Catholic vote and an unusually large percentage of the Jewish vote. Reagan made deep inroads into the blue-collar and union vote, which any Democrat must have to win the presidency. Independents, the swing voters that both parties court, went to Reagan by more than a five-to-three margin. Even one-third of the registered Democrats deserted their party in this election.

The only large groups whose support for Carter stayed firm were blacks and Hispanics, but smaller numbers of them voted in 1980 than in 1976.

Did the Reagan landslide carry over to GOP candidates in gubernatorial and congressional races?

Yes. The Republicans made a net gain of four governorships to bring their total to 23. The new GOP governors were Frank White in Arkansas, Christopher Bond in Missouri, Allen Olson in North Dakota, and John Spellman in Washington. For the Republican gains in Congress see Chapter 14.

Did more people vote in 1980 than in any previous presidential election?

Yes. About 86.5 million Americans cast their ballots in 1980. This was nearly 5 million more voters than in 1976, the year with the second largest turnout.

Was the proportion of voters to the total adult population also larger in 1980 than in previous presidential elections?

No. The proportion of voters declined in each of the five presidential elections between 1964 and 1980.

Election year	%
1960	63.1
1964	61.8
1968	60.7
1972	55.4
1976	54.4
1980	53.2

Not since 1948, when the voter turnout was only 51.1 percent, has there been a smaller proportion of voters than there was in 1980.

Why did the Associated Press rent a tree during the campaign?

The media needed command posts near Reagan's home in Pacific Palisades. ABC rented a nearby garage and NBC a one-room apartment. CBS installed a telephone jack near a fence across the street. The Associated Press rented a tree to which it strapped a locked box with a telephone for reporters to use.

Between 1900 and 1980 there were 21 presidential elections. Did Republicans or Democrats win more of these elections?

The Republicans and Democrats had the same number of wins before 1980 but Ronald Reagan's victory gave the GOP an 11-10 lead in presidential elections held during the twentieth century.

Republicans had cause to celebrate after the 1980 presidential election. In Chapter 9 other GOP landslide victories in earlier years are discussed.

How is the number of electoral votes determined?

To reach the total of 538 electoral votes, one is allotted for every congressman (435) and every senator (100), plus the three electoral votes that were given to the District of Columbia by the 23rd Amendment in 1961.

Does the number of each state's electoral votes change?

Yes. After each Census is taken every ten years, the new population figures are used to reapportion the number of congressional seats to which each state is entitled. A state may gain or lose seats in Congress, depending on whether since the last Census it gained or lost population relative to the other states. When a population change causes a state to have more or less congressional representatives, it also will have more or less electoral votes.

California, for example, has had a greatly expanding population in the twentieth century, and this accounts for its increasing number of electoral votes. In 1900 California had only 9 electoral votes. By 1932 it had 22 electoral votes, and this figure jumped to 32 in 1952, to 40 in 1964, and to 45 in the elections from 1972 through 1980. New York, on the other hand, has lost electoral votes steadily since 1948 when it had 47. In 1952 its electoral vote total dropped to 45, in 1964 to 43, and in 1972 to 41. Since 1972 California, rather than New York, has been the biggest prize in presidential elections. Since Reagan was popular in California, his home state, this helps explain why he almost won the Republican nomination in 1976 and did win it in 1980.

Why did congressional reapportionment based on the 1980 Census seem to improve Republican prospects to retain the White House for the rest of this decade?

Because, in general, the states that gained electoral votes in 1984 are in the Republican-dominated Sunbelt region, while the states losing electoral votes are in the Democratically-strong Frostbelt region. The chart below shows that since 1980 there were 17 more electoral votes distributed among 11 states, all of which Ronald Reagan carried in 1980.

Electoral Votes

	1980	1984	Net change
Alabama	9	9	
Alaska	3	3	
Arizona	6	7	plus 1
Arkansas	6	6	
California	45	47	plus 2
Colorado	7	8	plus 1
Connecticut	8	8	
Delaware	3	3	
D.C.	3	3	
Florida	17	21	plus 4
Georgia	12	12	
Hawaii	4	4	
Idaho	4	4	
Illinois	26	24	minus 2
Indiana	13	12	minus 1
Iowa	8	8	
Kansas	7	7	
Kentucky	9	9	
Louisiana	10	10	
Maine	4	4	
Maryland	10	10	
Massachusetts	14	13	minus 1
Michigan	21	20	minus 1

Minnesota	10	10	
Mississippi	7	7	
Missouri	12	11	minus 1
Montana	4	4	
Nebraska	5	5	
Nevada	3	4	plus 1
New Hampshire	4	4	
New Jersey	17	16	minus 1
New Mexico	4	5	plus 1
New York	41	36	minus 5
No. Carolina	13	13	
No. Dakota	3	3	
Ohio	25	23	minus 2
Oklahoma	8	8	
Oregon	6	7	plus 1
Pennsylvania	27	25	minus 2
Rhode Island	4	4	
So. Carolina	8	8	
So. Dakota	4	3	minus 1
Tennesee	10	11	plus 1
Texas	26	29	plus 3
Utah	4	5	plus 1
Vermont	3	3	
Virginia	12	12	
Washington	9	10	plus 1
West Virginia	6	6	
Wisconsin	11	11	
Wyoming	3	3	

BATTLE FOR
THE WHITE HOUSE, 1984

Who was the last major candidate—Democrat or Republican—to announce his intentions to run for the presidency in 1984?

President Ronald Reagan, who entered the race on January 29, 1984. All of the eight major Democratic contenders had tossed their hats in the ring in 1983.

As the 1984 campaign approached, why did the remarkable increase of voters in the 1982 congressional elections trouble Republicans?

Nearly 10 million more Americans voted for House elections in 1982 than had voted in 1978, the most recent previous midterm congressional election. In 1982 the vote for Democratic House candidates rose by more than six million, while the vote for Republican House candidates increased by only three million.

Why did the "gender gap" also concern the Republicans?

Women have cast more ballots than men in every presidential election since 1964, and it was thought that in 1984 several million more women than men might go to the polls. In the 1980 election men voters preferred Ronald Reagan to Jimmy Carter by 56 to 36 percent, but women gave Reagan only a scant 47-to-45 percent margin of their votes. Two years later, exit polls showed that women favored Democratic congressional candidates over Republicans by 21 percent, and in 1982 women provided the margins that elected three new Democratic governors—James Blanchard of Michigan, Mark White of Texas, and Mario Cuomo of New York.

Traditionally, have Republican presidential candidates appealed more to men than to women?

No. Between 1920, when nationwide woman suffrage began, and 1980 women gave a larger percentage of their votes to Republicans than did men in every presidential election except two: 1964, when Lyndon B. Johnson defeated Barry Goldwater, and 1980.

What action taken by the 1984 Democratic convention was applauded by many feminist groups?

The Democrats nominated Congresswoman Geraldine A. Ferraro of New York as the vice-presidential running mate of former Vice-President Walter F. Mondale.

Immediately after its convention a political party usually enjoys at least a brief upward surge in the polls. Did this happen after the 1984 Democratic convention?

Yes. In a July 13–16 preconvention Gallup Poll Reagan led Mondale by 53 to 39 percent, but on July 20, the day after the Democratic convention adjourned, a new Gallup Poll showed that Mondale had taken a narrow 48 to 46 percent lead. A Harris survey also found the two tickets virtually tied in a poll taken during the five days after the convention. However, by July 30 Gallup reported that Reagan had regained his lead by a margin of 53 to 41 percent.

Usually presidential candidates do little or no campaigning between the end of the conventions and Labor Day. Was this true also in 1984?

No. On July 25, less than a week after the Democratic convention and nearly a month before the Republican convention, President Reagan launched the opening salvo of his reelection campaign in Austin, Texas, charging that the Democratic leaders "have moved so far left, they've left America." The President also visited Georgia and New Jersey on this early campaign swing. Meanwhile, Walter Mondale and Geraldine Ferraro started campaigning on July 31 at Cleveland, Ohio, and then addressed rallies in Mississippi and Texas.

Where was the 1984 Republican convention?

In Dallas, Texas, which in 1984 hosted its first national convention for either major political party.

Who was the keynote speaker at the Republican convention?

Katherine D. Ortega, the United States treasurer, who was the first woman keynote speaker at a national Republican convention.

Did other prominent women address the convention?

Yes. Among the women who spoke at the convention were Transportation Secretary Elizabeth Hanford Dole, U.N. Ambassador Jeane J. Kirkpatrick, and Health and Human Services Secretary Margaret Heckler. Following a film tribute to her, Nancy Reagan also made a brief appearance at the rostrum and urged the TV audience to "make it one more time for the Gipper."

At the convention Republicans nominated Ronald Reagan for a second term by a nearly unanimous vote (two delegates abstained). When was the last time that an incumbent President won renomination without at least token opposition?

In 1956, when Dwight D. Eisenhower was nominated for a second term.

In his speech accepting the presidential nomination, what did Reagan mean when he said that the 1984 election presented the nation with "the clearest political choice of a half century"?

Reagan declared that "the choices this year are not just between two different personalities or between two different political parties, but between two fundamentally different ways of governing—their government of pessimism, fear, and limits . . . or ours of hope, confidence, and growth."

Why did Reagan go to Orange County in California for his formal campaign kickoff on Labor Day?

Because in 1980 Orange County had given Reagan his largest victory margin of any county in the United States. He had defeated President Jimmy Carter in Orange County by 68 to 23 percent, with a 9 percent scattering for other candidates.

In August 1981 President Reagan signed into law two important economic bills that had major repercussions in his 1984 campaign for reelection. What did these laws do?

One law reduced government spending on domestic programs by $130 billion over three years. The other law cut taxes by $750 billion over five years.

In spite of the large slashes in government spending for domestic programs, why did the federal budget deficit increase enormously during the Reagan administration?

The spiraling budget deficit was caused mainly by the large reduction in taxes, the massive defense buildup to match the Soviet Union's military strength, and the burgeoning interest that had to be paid on the growing deficit.

How did possible tax raises become a major campaign issue in 1984?

In his acceptance speech at the Democratic convention, Walter Mondale asserted that following the election, taxes would have to be raised to decrease the deficit, but that President Reagan would not admit this to the American public. The President replied that he was strongly against raising taxes and would take such action "only as a last resort." The GOP party platform declared even more emphatically that Republicans would "categorically reject proposals to increase taxes in a misguided effort to balance the budget."

Since Republicans opposed raising taxes, how did they plan to reduce the budget deficit?

The GOP platform said that the deficit would be reduced by cutting waste in government and by adhering to Reagan's financial policies, which will continue the "strong economic recovery" and thus increase the number of tax-paying individuals and companies. The platform also called for a constitutional amendment requiring a balanced budget.

How did Democrats and Republicans disagree about the domestic spending cuts in the Reagan administration?

Democrats charged that millions of Americans had been hurt by the scaling down of such government programs as food stamps, free school lunches, student loans, Aid to Families with Dependent Children, Medicaid, and Social Security payments to disabled persons. Republicans responded that since the New Deal (and especially since Lyndon B. Johnson's Great Society program), the nation had gone much too far in the direction of creating a welfare state, and the time had come to reverse this trend which had become increasingly costly to the taxpayers.

President Reagan strongly believed that the policies of his administration had greatly improved the nation's overall economy. How could he make this claim?

"When I was elected I promised to do five things," Reagan said. "Cut taxes. Reduce civilian spending. Restrain and stabilize monetary growth. Get rid of excessive regulation. And balance the budget. Now," he added, "I'm batting four out of five so far, and that's .800—pretty good hitting in any league that I know about." The President also took some credit for the sharp drop in inflation, which plunged from 11.7 percent in 1981 to 4.2 percent in 1984, and for the nation's most powerful economic expansion since the Korean War.

What remarks made by Reagan at a Dallas prayer breakfast brought religion into the campaign?

Reagan declared that "religion and politics are necessarily related" and "this has worked to our benefit as a nation." These statements led Mondale to question whether the President believed in the separation of church and state. Mondale asserted that "most Americans would be surprised to learn that God is a Republican" and condemned what he called "the rise of moral McCarthyism."

How did Reagan respond to these charges?

While he praised a "new spiritual awareness" in the nation, the President declared that "the United States of America is, and must remain, a nation of openness to people of all beliefs . . . . The ideals of our country leave no room whatsoever for intolerance, anti-Semitism, or bigotry of any kind—none. The unique thing about America is a wall in our Constitutuion separating church and state."

How did the candidates differ on the question of prayer in schools?

Reagan said that one of the reasons for his decision to seek reelection was to advance "the need to bring God back into the schools." He supported a constitutional amendment permitting voluntary prayer in school and accused its opponents of being "intolerant of religion."

Mondale took the position that students can pray whenever they wish but there should be no organized prayers in classrooms. "A President," he said, "must not let it be thought that political dissent from him is un-Christian."

How did Reagan and Mondale disagree on the abortion issue?

Reagan supported the so-called right-to-life constitutional amendment to ban abortion, while Mondale opposed the amendment, saying that the decision on abortion "essentially has to be a judgment made by people in their own lives on the basis of their own faith."

What position did Geraldine Ferraro, a Catholic, take on abortion?

She personally opposed abortion but said her religious beliefs did not affect her conduct in public office and that she supported the 1973 Supreme Court decision permitting abortion. Her position was attacked by various Catholic clergymen and often led to protests by right-to-life supporters at her political rallies.

Did most evangelical fundamentalist Protestant groups, such as the Moral Majority, support Reagan in 1984?

Yes. They generally agreed with Reagan's views and vowed to register many new voters for the Republican cause. Mondale was concerned that these religious groups were "reaching for government power to impose their own beliefs on other people. And the Reagan administration has opened its arms to them."

Why was the future course of the Supreme Court an issue in the 1984 presidential election?

Five of the nine justices were 75 or older, so there was a strong likelihood that the man elected to the White House in 1984 would be filling several vacancies on the Supreme Court.

Revelations about the finances of Geraldine Ferraro and her husband, John Zaccaro, undoubtedly hurt the Democrats' cause. Who was the last previous vice-presidential candidate to have his finances questioned?

Richard Nixon, whose contributions from wealthy constituents led to his famous "Checkers" speech in 1952.

What former gold medal winner in the Olympics was a third-party presidential candidate in 1984?

Bob Richards, the winner of gold medals in the Olympics pole vault in 1952 and 1956, was the presidential candidate of the newly revived Populist Party, which in 1984 merged with the American Independent Party. The last presidential candidate of the old Populist Party, which flourished in the 1890's, was Thomas E. Watson of Georgia, who polled 28,376 votes in 1908.

Did John Anderson, who had run as an independent presidential candidate in 1980, enter the 1984 race?

No. Anderson endorsed Walter Mondale in the 1984 election.

What positions did the presidential candidates take regarding the Equal Rights Amendment?

Reagan opposed it, and Mondale favored it.

How did the candidates differ on improving education?

Mondale said he would seek more federal funds to improve schools by attracting and keeping good teachers, modernizing laboratories, and strengthening graduate studies. He also wanted more college loans for the less affluent students and more government support for the education of minorities and needy children. Reagan believed that state governments should take the lead in promoting educational reforms and that federal funds should be reserved primarily for the disadvantaged and handicapped.

Reagan favored and Mondale opposed tuition tax credits to parents of private-school pupils. Reagan supported merit pay for superior teachers, but Mondale did not endorse merit pay, which is a controversial issue in teacher organizations.

Polls showed what age group gave Reagan his strongest support?

In poll after poll, Reagan ran strongest not among his fellow senior citizens or even middle-aged voters. Instead, his popularity was greatest among those who were 18 to 24 years old. A poll taken for *Time* in early October showed Reagan leading Mondale among the youngest voters by an astounding margin of 45 points, 63 percent to 18 percent. Voters in the 25-to-34 age group provided the second largest margin, with Reagan ahead of Mondale by 56 percent to 24 percent.

The chief reasons given for Reagan's enormous popularity with young people were the improving economy, including the prospect of more jobs, and the perception of the President as a strong, resolute leader.

When Reagan ran for the presidency in 1980, he promised to "rearm America." To what extent was this promise kept?

President Reagan presided over the largest peacetime military buildup in United States history. Annual defense spending increases, when adjusted for inflation, averaged about 10 percent between 1981 and 1984. The Reagan administration's "strategic modernization" program called for such major defense items as the 10-warhead MX intercontinental ballistic missile (ICBM), the single-warhead mobile ICBM called the "midgetman," the B-1 bomber, and submarines with nuclear missiles. Also, over the next five years the administration planned to spend about $25 billion on space-based antimissile defenses (dubbed "Star Wars" by opponents).

What national defense program did Mondale advocate?

Promising a military defense that would be "smart, lean, and tough," Mondale said that if elected President he would install a Pentagon budget that would increase by 3 or 4 percent a year but would total $25 billion less than the Reagan administration projected through 1989. Mondale would drop the MX missile, the B-1 bomber, and plans for space-based missile defenses. He would support ground-based and air-launched cruise missiles, the "stealth" bomber, new Trident submarine-launched nuclear missiles, and the ICBM "midgetman."

How did Mondale and Reagan differ in regard to dealing with the Soviet Union?

Mondale favored a mutually verifiable nuclear weapons freeze. Reagan opposed such a freeze but offered tradeoffs in the reduction of key weapons as a first step in slowing the arms race. Mondale committed himself to a U.S.-Soviet summit meeting within six months of taking office and to subsequent annual meetings. Reagan proposed a step-by-step approach to summitry, with Cabinet-level meetings preparing the way, which, he said, would enhance the possibility that a summit meeting would be productive.

What issue in Central America provoked the sharpest disagreement between Reagan and Mondale?

The issue of helping the CIA-supported Nicaraguan rebels to keep attacking the left-wing Sandinistas that are supported by Communist countries. Praising these *contra* rebels as freedom fighters, Reagan wanted the United States to continue sending them aid. Mondale argued that the United States should not be involved in covert actions to help the rebels. Also, he criticized our mining Nicaraguan harbors and the publication of a CIA manual that he said endorsed the assassination of Sandinista leaders.

What did Congresswoman Patricia Schroeder mean when she called Reagan the "Teflon President"?

She meant that nothing bad seemed to stick to the President.

The first televised debate between Reagan and Mondale occurred on October 7. What were the chief issues discussed?

This debate in Louisville featured domestic issues, including taxation, budget and trade deficits, Social Security, abortion, the role of religion in politics, and school prayer.

Which candidate did the public perceive as "winning" this debate?

Most polls indicated that the public was more favorably impressed by Mondale's performance. He was perceived as poised and confident, aggressive but still respectful, and well informed about the issues. Reagan was viewed as uncharacteristically ill at ease, hesitant and rambling in some of his remarks, and perhaps tiring in the last half-hour of the 90-minute debate.

What reasons did Reagan's aides give for his disappointing performance?

They said that the President had been besieged with too

many statistics in preparation for the debate and had been subjected to several long, grueling rehearsals. Moreover, the challenger in a presidential debate always has the advantage of being able to attack the incumbent's record, which tends to put the President on the defensive. Also, Mondale had gained experience from participating in many debates before winning the Democratic presidential nomination, while Reagan had faced no opposition in his party and could have been rusty in debating techniques.

How did each political camp react to this first debate?

Before the debate Mondale was trailing Reagan badly in all the polls, with some showing him more than 20 points behind and losing in nearly every state. So Democrats hailed Mondale's strong showing in the first debate as providing needed momentum for his sagging campaign. They felt it also raised a new election ` issue—Reagan's age (73) and his mental alertness to cope with problems in the White House.

Republican leaders, on the other hand, declared that Mondale had not delivered a "knockout blow," which they said was necessary if he had any chance to hurt the President's campaign for reelection.

Vice-presidential candidates George Bush and Geraldine Ferraro had their only debate on October 11. Was there much difference between men and women in their reactions to this debate?

Yes. An ABC News poll taken an hour after the debate showed that Bush was the choice of 46 percent of the male viewers to 29 percent for Ferraro, but women viewers gave the edge to Ferraro, 38 percent to 37 percent. In a Gannett Poll Bush was seen as the winner by 59 percent of the men to 18 percent for Ferraro, with 19 percent calling it a tie. Among women, however, it was almost even—39 percent for Bush, 38 percent for Ferraro, with 16 percent saying it was a tie.

On October 12 Reagan copied what previous President when he campaigned from the back of a railway car that passed through several Ohio towns?

Reagan used the same railway car and traveled the same route that Harry Truman did during his victorious "give 'em hell" reelection race in 1948. Perhaps regretting that he had not thought of this tactic, Mondale called Reagan's railroad trip the "Great Train Robbery."

The second and final presidential debate, on October 21, focused on what subjects?

National defense and foreign affairs.

Did Reagan or Mondale "win" this second debate?

This debate was judged to be much closer than the first encounter, with most polls giving a slight edge to Reagan. Probably the most important effect of the second debate was that Reagan's strong performance reduced concerns about the President's advanced age and convinced many television viewers that he was still an able leader and the "Great Communicator."

Reagan tried to turn the question of his age into an advantage by what quip that he made in the second debate?

The 73-year-old President said, ". . . I will not make age an issue of this campaign. I am not going to exploit for political purposes my opponent's youth and inexperience."

How did the two Reagan-Mondale debates affect the candidates' standings in the polls?

Following the first debate Mondale narrowed Reagan's lead in most polls by a few percentage points, but after the second debate Reagan regained his huge lead, which continued to increase during the last two weeks of the campaign.

On the day before the election did any major poll show that Reagan was in danger of losing the race?

No. Reagan led in the Gallup Poll by 18 points (which was the actual margin by which he won the election). Other major polls showed the President leading by 10 to 25 points.

On November 6, 1984, Ronald Reagan won a spectacular victory that stretched from coast to coast. How many states were in his victory column?

Reagan carried 49 states, losing only Minnesota and the District of Columbia to Mondale.

How close did Reagan come to making the election a 50-states sweep?

Reagan lost Minnesota by about 15,000 votes out of more than 2 million votes cast.

Reagan amassed 525 electoral votes to 13 for Mondale. Has any other Republican presidential candidate in history ever won that many electoral votes?

No. The runner-up was Richard Nixon, who won 520 electoral votes in the 1972 election against George McGovern.

Did Walter Mondale win fewer electoral votes than any other Democratic presidential candidate in history?

Yes. (McGovern won 17 electoral votes in 1972.) But the record for the lowest electoral-vote totals in this century is shared by two Republicans: William Howard Taft in 1912 and Alfred M. Landon in 1936. Each won only two states and eight electoral votes.

In 1980 Utah provided Reagan's largest winning margin over Jimmy Carter. Did this happen again in 1984?

Yes, but in 1984 Reagan captured 75 percent of the vote in Utah compared with 72 percent in 1980.

What three other states did Reagan win with at least 70 percent of the vote?

Idaho, Nebraska, and Wyoming.

What six other states did Reagan carry by more than a two-to-one margin?

Alaska, Arizona, Kansas, Nevada, New Hampshire, and Oklahoma.

Reagan won what state that never before had been carried by a Republican, except by Richard Nixon in 1972?

Hawaii.

What three other states that voted Democratic in five of the last six presidential elections also were captured by Reagan?

Maryland, Massachusetts, and Rhode Island. However, these

three states gave Reagan his narrowest winning margins. He carried Massachusetts with about 51 percent of the vote and Maryland and Rhode Island with about 52 percent.

Walter Mondale won a slim victory in his home state of Minnesota. How close did the Democrats come to winning Geraldine Ferraro's home state of New York?

The Democrats lost New York by 46 percent to 54 percent.

Did Ronald Reagan and George Bush win their home states by impressive margins?

Yes. They carried California by 58 percent to 42 percent and Texas by 64 percent to 36 percent.

Was the gender gap evident, as expected, in the election results?

Yes, but the Republicans still carried the vote of both sexes. Men voted 62 percent for the Reagan-Bush ticket and 38 percent for Mondale and Ferraro, while women chose the GOP candidates over the Democrats by 54 percent to 46 percent.

How large was the margin that white voters gave to the Republican ticket?

Reagan and Bush won the white vote by an astonishing 63 percent to 37 percent.

Jimmy Carter in 1980 also won less than half of the white vote. How long has it been since the Democratic presidential candidate won a majority of the white vote?

The last Democratic presidential candidate to win more than half of the white vote was Lyndon B. Johnson in 1964.

Did black voters support Mondale in overwhelming numbers?

Yes. Mondale won about 91 percent of the black vote nationwide and 86 percent of the vote in the heavily black District of Columbia.

Did Reagan attract a higher Hispanic vote in 1984 or 1980?

Reagan won 44 percent of the Hispanic vote in 1984 but only 37 percent in 1980.

By how large a margin did the Republican ticket capture the 1984 Protestant vote?

Although the fathers of Walter Mondale and his wife both were Protestant ministers, the Republicans won the Protestant vote by a whopping 66 percent to 34 percent.

With Geraldine Ferraro, a Catholic, on their ticket were the Democrats able to salvage the Catholic vote?

No. Reagan won about 56 percent of the Catholic vote.

Did Mondale carry the Jewish vote?

Yes. Mondale won the Jewish vote by 69 percent to 31 percent, which was a few percentage points higher than Carter's Jewish vote in 1980.

Did the vote of independents split more than two-to-one in favor of the Republican ticket?

Yes.

Did Mondale win the vote of people in the lowest income groups?

Yes. Mondale won the majority of families earning less than $10,000 a year, but Reagan carried all of the groups with an annual income of $10,000 or more.

Did Reagan make deep inroads into the union vote?

Yes. Despite his strong support from the AFL-CIO and teacher groups, Mondale won the union vote by only about 55 percent to 45 percent.

Was there any region of the country that voted more solidly for Reagan than the other regions?

Yes. Reagan carried the South with 62 percent of the vote, the West with 60 percent, the Midwest with 58 percent, and even the Northeast with 55 percent.

Was Reagan victorious among all age groups?

Yes. He swept every age group by a margin of about three-to-two, but his lead in the age group under 30 was smaller than some polls had predicted.

Did Reagan's landslide help to produce huge GOP victories in the 1984 gubernatorial and congressional elections?

No, the Reagan landslide did not spill over to the gubernatorial and congressional races, which led some analysts to conclude that Reagan's huge victory was mainly a personal triumph for a very popular President rather than an indication that the GOP had emerged as the nation's dominant political party.

In 13 gubernatorial races the Republicans won only one additional statehouse. They elected four new governors in North Carolina, Rhode Island, Utah, and West Virginia, but the GOP lost its governors' seats in North Dakota, Washington, and Vermont. Republicans also fell short of their goals in congressional races. (See pages 181-182.)

What factors accounted for Reagan's enormous personal victory at the polls?

It is very difficult to unseat any incumbent President during a period of relative peace and prosperity. Reagan won a second term in the White House partly because of the solid accomplishments of his first term—lower taxes, lower inflation, lower interest rates, more purchasing power; greater national pride and a resurgent dedication to spiritual and family values; an increased national defense and the refusal to be intimidated by the Soviets. Moreover, the huge size of the President's vote obviously was enhanced by his personal qualities. Many voters perceived Reagan as a strong, effective leader, as the most charismatic and ennobling communicator in the White House since John F. Kennedy, as a President committed to championing personal initiative and to ending government expenditures to those who are not truly needy, and as a persistent prophet of optimism who envisions a bright future for Americans in their quest for a "shining city on a hill."

Reagan's decisive win was due in part also to the Democrats' flaws and failures. The intense intraparty rivalry among Walter Mondale, Gary Hart, and Jesse Jackson left deep wounds that were hard to heal; Mondale was accused of being the puppet of special interest groups, especially labor unions; the financial problems of Geraldine Ferraro hurt the Democrats' cause, and Mondale's candid demand for higher taxes was unpopular with many voters. Also, Mondale failed to articulate any issue that caught fire with the public, and he was burdened by his close association with the largely unsuccessful Carter administration.

How many times in the history of our two major political parties has a Vice-President who was defeated for reelection (which happened to Mondale in 1980) been his party's presidential nominee four years later?
This has never occurred before.

On election night a grateful Ronald Reagan spoke on television to a national audience. With what optimistic remark did he end his victory speech?
"You ain't seen nothin' yet!"

About how many people voted in 1984?
The total vote in 1984 was about 92 million, which was an increase of about 5.5 million over the vote in 1980. Still, about 47 percent of the total adult population did not vote. This means that nearly half of all eligible Americans squandered the most precious right that people who live in a democracy have.

*   *   *   *

The next four chapters discuss the results of presidential elections since 1856, when the rivalry between the Democratic and Republican parties began.

LANDSLIDE VICTORIES

The only thing better than a close victory at the
polls is to win by a landslide. . .

How much larger was Reagan's 1984 landslide over Mondale than his 1980 landslide over Carter?

In 1984 Ronald Reagan won 49 states; in 1980 he won 44 states. Reagan gained 36 more electoral votes in 1984 than in 1980. Also, his share of the popular vote was about 59 percent in 1984 and about 51 percent in 1980.

Of all the candidates since George Washington, who won the most votes in a presidential election?

Ronald Reagan, who got about 53.5 million votes in 1984.

What percent of the popular vote constitutes a landslide victory in an election with only two major candidates?

If one candidate has more than 54 percent of the popular vote, this is often considered a landslide victory. But in a race with three or more strong candidates, one of them can win by a landslide with a much smaller percent of the popular vote, as Ronald Reagan did in 1980.

Who had the highest percent of the popular vote of any Republican candidate in a presidential race?

In 1972 Richard Nixon had a higher percent of the popular vote than any other Republican nominee in history. His Democratic opponent, Senator George McGovern of South Dakota, carried only one state, Massachusetts, and the District of Columbia.

1972 Election	% of popular vote	Electoral votes
Richard Nixon (R)	60.69	520
George McGovern (D)	37.53	17

(The popular vote does not total 100 percent because a small percent of the vote went to minority-party candidates. The electoral votes do not add up to 538 because one individual elector, who was pledged to Nixon, voted instead for the Libertarian Party candidate.)

One of the largest Republican landslides occurred when joining the League of Nations was a major issue with American voters. Who was the GOP winner that year?

Senator Warren G. Harding of Ohio, who defeated Governor James M. Cox, also of Ohio, in 1920.

1920 Election	% of popular vote	Electoral votes
Warren G. Harding (R)	60.30	404
James M. Cox (D)	34.17	127

Another large Republican landslide was in 1928 when voters continued to support the "party of prosperity." Who was the victorious Republican candidate in that election?

Secretary of Commerce Herbert Hoover in 1928 swept to a smashing triumph over the Democratic governor of New York, Alfred E. Smith.

1928 Election	% of popular vote	Electoral votes
Herbert Hoover (R)	58.20	444
Alfred E. Smith (D)	40.77	87

Who was the first Republican nominee to achieve two landslide victories in the popular-vote count?

General Dwight D. Eisenhower, who twice defeated Adlai Stevenson of Illinois. Notice that in the rematch between these two contenders Eisenhower defeated Stevenson by a larger margin than he did in their first encounter.

1952 Election	% of popular vote	Electoral votes
Dwight D. Eisenhower (R)	55.13	442
Adlai Stevenson (D)	44.38	89

1956 Election		
Dwight D. Eisenhower (R)	57.37	457
Adlai Stevenson (D)	41.97	73

In the first decade of this century what former Vice-President won by a huge margin in his bid for a four-year term in the White House?

Theodore Roosevelt overwhelmed a colorless New York judge, Alton B. Parker, in the 1904 election.

1904 Election	%of popular vote	Electoral votes
Theodore Roosevelt (R)	56.41	336
Alton B. Parker (D)	37.60	140

What Republican President, in his race for reelection, triumphed easily over an opponent who ran both as a Democrat and a Liberal Republican?

Ulysses S. Grant swamped publisher Horace Greeley at the polls in 1872, even though Greeley was the candidate of both the Democratic Party and the anti-Grant Liberal Republicans.

1872 Election	% of popular vote	Electoral votes
Ulysses S. Grant (R)	55.63	286
Horace Greeley (D, LR)	43.83	0*

*Greeley died between the date when the voters cast their ballots in November and the time the electors voted in December, so his electors split their votes among four noncandidates.

What wartime President was reelected by a landslide over one of his former generals?

In 1864 Abraham Lincoln defeated General George McClellan by a much larger margin than he had anticipated. This was the one election when the Republican Party called itself the Union Party to appeal for support to northern Democrats who backed the Union cause.

1864 Election	% of popular vote	Electoral votes
Abraham Lincoln (R)	55.02	212
George McClellan (D)	44.96	21

When was the only time that a Republican presidential candidate faced a strong third-party opponent, as well as the Democratic challenger, and still won with more than 54 percent of the popular vote?

This was in 1924 when Calvin Coolidge defeated Democrat John W. Davis and the Progressive candidate, Robert M. LaFollette, who polled nearly 5 million votes but carried only his home state, Wisconsin.

1924 Election	% of popular vote	Electoral votes
Calvin Coolidge (R)	54.04	382
John W. Davis (D)	28.84	136
Robert M. LaFollette (P)	16.56	13

Why is it possible for a candidate to win a landslide in the electoral vote without necessarily winning a landslide in the popular vote?

When one candidate wins nearly all of the large states (with their big blocs of electoral votes) by narrow margins, he can acquire a huge number of electoral votes without necessarily having a proportionate share of the popular vote. A good example of this was the 1868 election in which General Ulysses S. Grant had almost three times as many electoral votes as Democrat Horatio Seymour had, yet Grant won in the popular vote by only about 5 percent.

1868 Election	% of popular vote	Electoral votes
Ulysses S. Grant (R)	52.66	214
Horatio Seymour (D)	47.34	80

What candidate won the electoral vote by a landslide, yet the percent of his popular vote was the smallest of any victorious Republican in the GOP's history?

In the 1860 election Abraham Lincoln had 57 more electoral votes than the combined total of three opponents, but he won the election with less than 40 percent of the popular vote.

1860 Election	% of popular vote	Electoral votes
Abraham Lincoln (R)	39.82	180
Stephen A. Douglas (D)	29.46	12
John C. Breckinridge (SD)	18.09	72
John Bell (CU)	12.61	39

Three out of every five voters did not want Lincoln as their President, yet he was elected because he carried the large Eastern and Midwestern states, generally by thin margins. His long-time rival, Stephen A. Douglas, ran a strong second in the states that Lincoln won, but Douglas captured only one state, Missouri, which explains his small number of electoral votes.

The Southern Democrats split the Democratic vote by refusing to support Douglas, and they ran Vice-President John C. Breckinridge of Kentucky as a purely sectional candidate. Breckinridge won 11 Southern states with 72 electoral votes, but he finished a poor third in the popular-vote column.

The fourth candidate, John Bell, represented the Constitutional Union Party, whose single goal was to keep the Union together and avert a war between the North and South. As expected, Bell ran strongest in the border states, where there was nearly an even number of Northern and Southern sympathizers. Bell carried three states—Kentucky, Tennessee, and Virginia.

After the Civil War started, what happened to the three states that Bell captured in the 1860 election?

Kentucky fought on the Union side, but its many slaveholders continued to keep their black people in bondage. Tennessee joined the Confederacy, but there were large pockets of Union supporters in the eastern part of the state, and Andrew Johnson refused to give up his Senate seat when Tennessee seceded. People in the western counties of Virginia refused to support the South, so in 1863 they seceded from their state and joined the Union as the new state of West Virginia.

Were there any states in 1860 where voters could not cast their ballots for Abraham Lincoln?

Yes, ironically, many American voters in 1860 could not cast their ballots for the man who is generally regarded as the greatest of all our Presidents. This was because Lincoln's name was not on the ballot in the Southern states of Alabama, Arkansas, Florida, Georgia, Louisiana, Mississippi, North Carolina, Tennessee, and Texas.

Why isn't South Carolina on the list of Southern states where voters could not cast their ballots for Lincoln?

Because in South Carolina the voters were not allowed to cast ballots for *any* presidential candidate until 1868. From 1789 until after the Civil War, South Carolina's presidential electors were selected by the state legislature, *not by the people.*

Colorful William Jennings Bryan was a thorn in the side of Republicans for many years. Was this three-time loser beaten by larger margins in the electoral vote or the popular vote?

In all three presidential elections Bryan was defeated more decisively in the electoral vote than in the popular vote. While Bryan carried 22 states to William McKinley's 23 states in 1896, Bryan still lost that election by 95 electoral votes. This was because McKinley won all the heavily populated Eastern states and most of the large Midwestern states, while Bryan gained only the sparsely populated Western states and a few Midwestern states.

Nevertheless, the Boy Orator of the Platte, as Bryan was called, proved to be a formidable campaigner. The figures on page 129 show that he held his Republican opponents to less than 52 percent of the popular vote in all three of his futile bids for the presidency.

1896 Election	% of popular vote	Electoral votes
William McKinley (R)	51.01	271
William Jennings Bryan (D,P*)	46.73	176

1900 Election		
William McKinley (R)	51.67	292
William Jennings Bryan (D)	45.51	155

1908 Election		
William H. Taft (R)	51.58	321
William Jennings Bryan (D)	43.05	162

*In the 1896 election Bryan was the candidate of both the Democratic and Populist parties.

CLIFF-HANGERS

A win is a win, no matter whether it is by a landslide
or a whisker. . .

In the last twenty years has any Republican presidential candidate won an election by less than 1 percent of the popular vote?

Yes, Richard Nixon won the 1968 election with a popular-vote margin of only .7 percent. Nixon defeated two strong challengers: Vice-President Hubert Humphrey, the Democratic candidate, and George Wallace, the former governor of Alabama and the candidate of his personally created American Independent Party. Segregationist Wallace captured five Southern states and 46 electoral votes. But of greater significance, he won nearly 10 million popular votes, setting a new record for third-party candidates.

1968 Election	% of popular vote	Electoral votes
Richard Nixon (R)	43.42	301
Hubert Humphrey (D)	42.72	191
George Wallace (AI)	13.53	46

While Nixon defeated Humphrey by 110 electoral votes in 1968, how might a few small shifts in voting have caused Nixon to lose the election?

The election results in a few states shown below suggest several ways that Nixon could have been denied a victory in the electoral college. Notice that in each of these states that Nixon carried, the combined votes for Humphrey and Wallace exceeded the number of votes for Nixon.

State	Electoral votes	Richard Nixon	Hubert Humphrey	George Wallace
California	40	3,467,664	3,244,318	487,270
Florida	14	886,804	676,794	624,207
Illinois	26	2,174,774	2,039,814	390,958
Missouri	12	811,932	791,444	206,126
New Jersey	17	1,325,467	1,264,206	262,187
Ohio	26	1,791,014	1,700,586	467,495
Wisconsin	12	809,997	748,804	127,835

If Humphrey had taken just 32 more electoral votes from Nixon, the election would have gone to the House of Representatives, which was controlled by the Democrats and almost certainly would have elected Humphrey. This could have happened if the Democrats had added to their win column the single state of California or any combination of states with an electoral-vote total of at least 32. Humphrey could have won the election outright if he had picked up 79 of Nixon's electoral votes. Had Nixon lost to Humphrey about 112,000 votes in California, about 68,000 votes in Illinois, and about 46,000 votes in Ohio, Humphrey would have won the election in a breeze—with 283 electoral votes to Nixon's 209. This change would have involved only about a quarter-million votes out of the 73 million that were cast!

In what presidential election did the Republican candidate have a winning popular-vote margin of only .02 percent?

In the 1880 election Congressman James A. Garfield of Ohio defeated General Winfield S. Hancock of Pennsylvania by the narrowest popular-vote margin in history. A total of 9,210,420 votes were cast, and Garfield's plurality was only 1,898 votes! The GOP nominee had a much wider lead in the electoral votes because he captured six of the seven most heavily populated states. Third-party candidate James B. Weaver of the Greenback Party polled over 300,000 votes, but he carried no states, and the votes cast for him did not affect the outcome of the results in any state, except possibly California.

1880 Election	% of popular vote	Electoral votes
James A. Garfield (R)	48.27	214
Winfield S. Hancock (D)	48.25	155
James B. Weaver (G)	3.32	0

What forgery may have caused Garfield to lose California in the 1880 election?

California had gone Republican in presidential elections from 1860 through 1876, but what could have been a string of six straight victories for the GOP was broken by a razor-thin Democratic win in 1880. This was partly due to a letter that severely damaged Garfield's campaign in the Golden State. Shortly before election day, a letter favoring additional Chinese immigration that was allegedly signed by Garfield was published in a New York newspaper. At that time many Californians were adamantly opposed to the influx of Chinese laborers in their state.

Garfield vehemently denied any knowledge of the letter and claimed that his signature had been forged. But this was only a few days before the election, and the damage to Garfield's candidacy in California could not be undone.

California	Garfield		Hancock		Weaver	
	votes	%	votes	%	votes	%
	80,282	48.9	80,426	49.0	3,381	2.1

In what presidential election did the Republican candidate win by a single electoral vote?

This was the famous "disputed" election of 1876 in which Republican Rutherford B. Hayes, governor of Ohio, defeated Democrat Samuel J. Tilden, governor of New York. On election day it appeared that Tilden had won the election. He led his GOP opponent by a quarter-million votes and captured 184 of the 185 electoral votes needed for victory. Hayes had only 166 electoral votes, 19 short of the magic number.

These 19 electoral votes, from the states of Florida, Louisiana, and South Carolina, were disputed. Each party vigorously claimed that its candidate had won all three of these Southern states. Tempers flared and tension heightened as the Republicans and Democrats angrily charged each other with attempted bribes, voter intimidation, stuffed and stolen ballot boxes, and falsified election returns.

Congress was forced to take some action, and finally it established a special 15-member electoral commission to investigate the disputes and decide how the electoral votes in each of the three states should be counted. The electoral commission included five congressmen, five senators, and five Supreme Court justices. Eight members of the commission were Republicans, seven were Democrats. Still, the Democratic Party leaders felt that the commission surely would agree with the evidence that Tilden had won the election, since even if he were given only one of the disputed states, that would have put him in the White House.

But on each of the disputes the commission voted along straight party lines, and by an 8-7 margin gave Hayes all the 19 electoral votes, thus withholding from Tilden the one precious vote that would have made him the first Democratic President since before the Civil War.

1876 Election	% of popular vote	Electoral votes
Rutherford B. Hayes (R)	47.95	185
Samuel J. Tilden (D)	50.97	184

In the 1876 election one man really decided who would be the next President. Who was this man?

When Congress originally appointed the electoral commission, it consisted of seven Republicans and seven Democrats. The fifteenth member was Justice David Davis, who was considered a political independent. Leaders of both parties felt that Davis would be unbiased and fair in reaching his decision on the disputed vote. But an unforeseen development occurred when the Illinois legislature named Davis to a seat in the Senate. Davis then resigned from the electoral commission, and his place was taken by Justice Joseph P. Bradley. Although Bradley was a Republican, the Democrats felt he would be less biased than any of the remaining justices, all of whom were also Republicans.

A delegation of Democratic leaders called on Bradley the night before the electoral commission was to vote on the disputes, and they came away from the meeting confident that Bradley's key vote would make Tilden the next President.

But the following morning Justice Joseph P. Bradley cast the decisive ballot that sent Hayes to the Executive Mansion.

How did it happen that the 1876 election nearly left the United States without a President?

Angry Democrats throughout the land raised a mighty storm of protest, charging that Tilden had been robbed of the presidency. In some areas they began gathering arms, forming volunteer companies, and threatening to start a second civil war if Hayes went to the White House.

In the meantime, the Democratic-controlled House of Representatives refused to accept the verdict of the electoral commission and· planned to filibuster so that the official electoral count could not be completed before inauguration day, March 4. If this happened, the United States would be without a President after the term of the outgoing Chief Executive expired the same day.

The haunting prospect of a leaderless country increased with every passing day. Finally, as inauguration day neared, the leaders of both parties agreed to a compromise. The Democrats would end the congressional filibuster and accept Hayes as President, while the Republicans promised to remove the last federal troops from the South, thus ending Reconstruction.

On March 2, 1877, the presiding officer of the Senate was able to announce that Hayes had been elected President. The new Chief Executive took his oath of office the following day because March 4 was a Sunday. The formal inauguration took place on March 5, and the crisis that could have led to another civil war was resolved.

Besides the 1876 election, was there any other presidential election in which the Republican winner had fewer popular votes than his Democratic opponent?

Yes, this happened again in 1888 when Benjamin Harrison took the White House away from the incumbent Democrat, Grover Cleveland. Although Cleveland had a plurality of over 90,000 votes, he failed to capture any of the four states that had more than 20 electoral votes—New York (36), Pennsylvania (30), Ohio (23), and Illinois (22). Harrison also carried all of New England except Connecticut, most of the Midwestern states, and all of the states west of Missouri except Texas.

Since Harrison won all of the four largest states and many of the smaller ones, why didn't he have more popular votes than Cleveland?

Because Harrison won most of his states by *slim* margins, while Cleveland won nearly all the Southern states by *huge* margins. Cleveland carried South Carolina with 82 percent of the popular vote, Louisiana and Mississippi with 73 percent, Georgia with 70 percent, and Alabama with 67 percent. Since Cleveland won the smaller Southern states by lopsided amounts, this offset Harrison's narrow victories in many closely contested states and enabled Cleveland to have more popular votes than the man who defeated him.

1888 Election	% of popular vote	Electoral votes
Benjamin Harrison (R)	47.82	233
Grover Cleveland (D)	48.62	168

In this close election what endorsement of Cleveland proved to be the "kiss of death"?

A Harrison supporter in California posed as a former British citizen and wrote the British minister in Washington, asking how he should vote in the upcoming presidential election. The naive British diplomat fell into the trap set for him. He answered that Queen Victoria's government would be delighted to see President Cleveland reelected. When the jubilant Californian received this reply, he hastened to have it printed in the newspaper. Publicizing the letter had the effect that its sly recipient desired. Cleveland was called the "British candidate," which infuriated large numbers of Irish voters who hated anything British. It's impossible to know how many Irish voted for Harrison because of this incident, but in heavily Irish Massachusetts the Republican vote jumped from 48.4 percent in 1884 to 53.4 percent in 1888. Even more important was what happened in New York, with its large number of Irish voters. The state had given its 36 electoral votes to Cleveland in 1884, but when the "British question" surfaced in 1888, Harrison took New York from Cleveland.

What happened when Harrison and Cleveland had their rematch in 1892?

Grover Cleveland was returned to the White House in 1892, but this election was strongly influenced by the Populist Party, whose candidate, James B. Weaver, made an impressive showing in Western mining states and Midwestern farm states. Weaver took most of his votes from former Republicans, and this played an important role in Cleveland's successful comeback. Weaver captured three states—Colorado, Kansas, and Nevada—that had voted Republican in 1888, plus the new state of Idaho that was participating in its first presidential election. In five other states that the Democrats won, the combined vote total for Harrison and Weaver was larger than Cleveland's winning margin.

California was one of the five states in which Weaver's candidacy may have tipped the scales away from Harrison and toward Cleveland. There couldn't be a much tighter race than the one California provided in 1892.

California	Cleveland		Harrison		Weaver	
	votes	%	votes	%	votes	%
	118,151	43.8	118,027	43.8	25,311	9.4

1892 Election	% of popular vote	Electoral votes
Benjamin Harrison (R)	42.96	145
Grover Cleveland (D)	46.05	277
James B. Weaver (P)	8.50	22

NEAR MISSES

As every Monday morning quarterback knows,
a narrow defeat prompts the plaintive refrain,
"Damn it, if only we had. . ."

How close did Gerald Ford come to defeating Jimmy Carter in 1976?

Shortly after the Democratic convention, Jimmy Carter, according to a Gallup Poll, had an unprecedented 33-point lead over the incumbent President. But during the fall campaign Gerald Ford whittled away at this nearly insurmountable lead. By November he had drawn even with his challenger, and the pollsters were saying that the race was too close to call.

The pollsters were right—when the ballots were counted, Carter had a bare 50.1 percent of the popular vote and only 27 more electoral votes than the 270 needed to win.

1976 Election	% of popular vote	Electoral votes
Jimmy Carter (D)	50.1	297
Gerald Ford (R)	48.0	240
Eugene McCarthy (I)*	0.9	0
Ronald Reagan**	0	1

*Former Senator Eugene McCarthy of Minnesota ran as an Independent candidate.
**A Ford elector from the state of Washington broke ranks and cast his electoral vote for noncandidate Ronald Reagan.

Carter carried four states by just a whisker. If Ford had taken Ohio (which he lost by about 11,000 votes out of more than 4 million cast) and one of these three other states, he would have been returned to the White House for another term:

State	Electoral votes	Carter	Ford	McCarthy
Hawaii	4	147,375	140,003	0
Mississippi	7	381,309	366,846	4,074
Ohio	25	2,011,621	2,000,505	58,258
Wisconsin	11	1,040,232	1,004,987	34,943

What court ruling during the 1976 campaign may have cost Ford the election?

A New York court ruled against permitting Independent Eugene McCarthy's name on the ballot in that state. McCarthy had a large liberal following in New York, but when his name was not on the ballot, it is believed that most of the liberals voted for Carter instead. Since Carter carried New York by less than 300,000 votes out of about 6,500,000, some political analysts contend that if McCarthy had been a candidate there, he would have drained enough votes away from Carter to give New York and the election to Ford.

Eugene McCarthy polled less than 1 percent of the popular vote and took no electoral votes, so did his candidacy make any significant difference in the election results?

No one can say for sure how McCarthy's supporters would have voted had he not been in the race, but it is very likely that Carter's victory would have been more substantial. In four states (with a total of 26 electoral votes) that were won by Ford, the combined Carter-McCarthy vote total was larger than Ford's.

State	Electoral votes	Carter	Ford	McCarthy
Iowa	8	619,931	632,863	20,051
Maine	4	232,279	236,320	10,874
Oklahoma	8	532,442	545,708	14,101
Oregon	6	490,407	492,120	40,207

What presidential election since World War II was an unusually bitter loss for Republicans because their candidate trailed the Democratic winner in the popular-vote count by only .17 percent?

In 1960 Senator John F. Kennedy nosed out Vice-President Richard Nixon with the smallest popular-vote margin in any presidential election since 1880. A record-breaking 68,828,960 Americans trooped to the polls, and the final tally showed Kennedy winning by 114,673 votes.

1960 Election	% of popular vote	Electoral votes
John F. Kennedy (D)	49.72	303
Richard Nixon (R)	49.55	219
Harry F. Byrd (D)*	0	15

*All of Mississippi's eight electors, together with six electors from Alabama and one from Oklahoma, cast their ballots for noncandidate Harry F. Byrd, a conservative Democratic senator from Virginia.

Kennedy captured three large states—Illinois, Missouri, and New Jersey, with a total of 56 electoral votes—and several smaller states by less than 1 percent of the popular vote. Only a small shift of votes in some of these states (Nixon lost Hawaii by 115 votes out of about 450,000) would have denied Kennedy the White House.

Why were Republicans especially aggravated by Nixon's loss in Illinois?

The race in Illinois was incredibly close:

Kennedy	Nixon	Margin of Kennedy's plurality
2,377,846	2,368,988	8,858

Republicans angrily charged that Boss Richard Daley's powerful Cook County machine rigged the ballot boxes in enough districts to provide Kennedy with his razor-thin victory in Illinois. The claims of fraud may have been exaggerated, but still it wouldn't have taken much political hanky-panky to shift about 4,500 votes out of nearly 4,750,000. Many Republicans, including most certainly Richard Nixon, never forgot what happened in Illinois in 1960.

Besides the 1960 election, have the Republicans lost any other presidential elections by less than 1 percent of the popular vote?

Yes. In 1884 only .25 percent of the popular vote separated the triumphant Democrat from the defeated Republican. The winner was Governor Grover Cleveland of New York; the loser was former House Speaker James G. Blaine of Maine.

The race for electoral votes was very close too, with New York playing the key role of the make-or-break state. Cleveland won New York, but if Blaine had taken that state, he would have had enough electoral votes to become the next President. More than 1,125,000 New Yorkers cast ballots, and Cleveland's winning margin was 1,047!

1884 Election	% of popular vote	Electoral votes
Grover Cleveland (D)	48.50	219
James G. Blaine (R)	48.25	182

How did the phrase "Rum, Romanism, and Rebellion" affect the outcome of the 1884 election?

Shortly before election day, Blaine was attending a reception hosted by a group of sympathetic Protestant ministers. One of the clergymen welcomed the candidate with the statement, "We are Republicans and don't propose to leave our party and identify ourselves with the party whose antecedents have been rum, Romanism, and rebellion." Undoubtedly, the naive minister thought that the last part of this sentence was nothing more than an alliterative way to express his support for Blaine.

But first the newspapers and then handbills from Democratic Party headquarters widely publicized "Rum, Romanism, and Rebellion" as a vicious insult to Roman Catholics. No apology from Blaine could undo the damage done by this insipid remark.

Without the modern techniques of surveying voter opinions, we can only guess how many Catholics were offended enough to switch their votes from Blaine to Cleveland. But "Rum, Romanism, and Rebellion" may have clinched New York for

Cleveland and assured him of becoming the first Democratic President since the Civil War.

What twentieth-century election was so close that the last state's returns determined the winner?

In the 1916 election President Woodrow Wilson ran for re-election against Charles E. Hughes, a Supreme Court justice. The betting odds favored Hughes, and the early returns indicated that he was the apparent winner. New York, Pennsylvania, New Jersey, and all of New England, except New Hampshire, were won by Hughes. The Republican candidate also carried the entire Midwest, with the exception of Ohio. All that Hughes still needed to win was California, and this Western state had not been taken by the Democrats in 24 years.

Because the returns from faraway California trickled in slowly, a couple of days passed before the final tally from that state could be recorded. But the newspapers already were reporting the election of Hughes, and on election night a cheering multitude of Republicans celebrated in Times Square. On the roof of New York's Hotel Astor, where the Republican nominee was staying, a giant electric sign flashed the name: "Hughes." Even Hughes's personal staff had started addressing their boss as "Mr. President-elect."

On Thursday afternoon, two days after the election, Hughes lay down for a nap and gave his secretary strict orders that he was not to be disturbed. While he was napping, a reporter phoned and asked to speak to Hughes.

"I'm sorry," replied the secretary, "but the President-elect is sleeping, and he cannot be disturbed."

"All right," grumbled the reporter, "but when Hughes wakes up tell him that he isn't the President-elect. The final returns from California just came in, and Wilson carried the state by about 3,400 votes."

California	Wilson	Hughes	Margin of Wilson's plurality
	465,936	462,516	3,420

To win the 1916 election a candidate needed 266 electoral votes. If Hughes had captured California's 13 votes, he would have gone to the White House with 1 more electoral vote than the required majority.

1916 Election	% of popular vote	Electoral votes
Woodrow Wilson (D)	49.24	277
Charles E. Hughes (R)	46.11	254

How did one small snub possibly cost Hughes the presidency?

For many years the most powerful figure in California politics was the Republican governor, Hiram Johnson. But some conservatives regarded Johnson as a dangerous maverick because he belonged to the progressive wing of the GOP and had deserted the party in 1912 to be Teddy Roosevelt's running mate on the "Bull Moose" ticket. William Crocker, the Republican national committeeman from California, wanted nothing to do with Johnson and his "radical" ideas.

At the same time that Hughes was running for President, Johnson was ending his reign as California's governor and seeking a Senate seat. One day when Hughes was campaigning in Long Beach, California, Johnson was staying at the same hotel. Political etiquette called for Crocker, who was shepherding Hughes around the state, to pay a courtesy call on the governor. But the meeting was never arranged, and Johnson angrily concluded that Hughes had snubbed him.

So Johnson sulked in his corner and refused to campaign for Hughes, even though the two men had much in common because Hughes had been a progressive governor of New York before his appointment to the Supreme Court.

In November when Californians cast their ballots, Hiram Johnson won his Senate seat by a whopping 300,000 votes, but when Republicans looked for his coattails Hughes was nowhere to be found.

Why did the 1948 presidential election provide the biggest surprise in our political history?

Republicans were supremely confident in 1948 that they would finally win the presidency—for the first time in 20 years. The GOP had regained control of Congress in 1946, and there were many signs that the mood of the public was taking a conservative turn.

The Democratic administration was besmirched by charges of corruption and accused of being soft on Communism. Moreover, the unbeatable and tremendously charismatic Franklin D. Roosevelt was dead, and his successor in the White House, Harry S Truman, was no carbon copy of FDR. Public opinion surveys gave the Truman administration very low marks and indicated that large numbers of Americans felt that the feisty little man with the steel-rimmed glasses and nasal Missouri twang was simply not fit to continue as President.

Then too, in 1948 the Democratic Party was in dreadful disarray and split into three warring factions. The left-wingers who felt the administration was too tough on Communist Russia created what they called the new Progressive Party and nominated former Vice-President Henry Wallace to run as their presidential candidate. To make matters even worse for Truman, Southern segregationists, unhappy with the party platform's strong stand on civil rights, bolted the Democratic convention and formed the States' Rights "Dixiecrat" Party. South Carolina Governor J. Strom Thurmond became their presidential nominee.

The Republican Party nominated an attractive pair of candidates, New York Governor Thomas E. Dewey for President and California Governor Earl Warren for Vice-President.

Pollsters were so certain that Dewey would win the election by a landslide that they quit sampling voters' opinions in mid-October. On election eve hardly any political leaders, except Truman himself, gave the Democratic incumbent even a slight chance of winning.

But the election results gave the Republicans apoplexy and Truman another term in the White House.

1948 Election	% of popular vote	Electoral votes
Harry S Truman (D)	49.51	303
Thomas E. Dewey (R)	45.12	189
J. Strom Thurmond (SR)	2.40	39
Henry Wallace (P)	2.38	0

"What happened?" pondered the shocked Republicans. Apparently many things didn't go according to form, but three stand out as particularly important: (1) The desertion from the Democratic ranks of the Wallace left-wingers and the Thurmond right-wingers may have helped Truman because he could then be perceived as a moderate, and most voters consider themselves moderates rather than extremists. (2) Not only were the Republicans vastly overconfident, but Dewey was too placid and proper (he never had one hair out of place) to fire the voters' imagination and too mild in his criticism of Truman to turn the campaign into an all-out GOP crusade. (3) President Truman pled his case convincingly in the heartland of America. Launching an effective "whistle-stop" campaign, he ordered that his train be stopped wherever groups of voters, large or small, had gathered. Then speaking from the rear platform in plain but forceful words, the President praised the Democrats' accomplishments and castigated the Republican-dominated 80th Congress as a "do-nothing" legislature.

The crowds warmed to Truman's folksy message and shouted back, "Give 'em hell, Harry"—which is exactly what the President did to his three opponents on the first Tuesday in November.

If Dewey had taken two states that Truman carried by razor-thin margins, the 1948 election would have been the first decided in the House of Representatives since 1825. What two states were they?

California and Ohio, each with 25 electoral votes. If these two states had gone into the Republican column, Truman's electoral-vote count would have been cut to 253, or 13 votes short of the 266 needed to win a majority. The figures below show how close the nation came to having its President selected by the House of Representatives.

State	Truman	Dewey	Margin of Truman's Plurality
California	1,913,134	1,895,269	17,865
Ohio	1,452,791	1,445,684	7,107

On the other hand, if Thurmond and Wallace had not run, would Truman have won more electoral votes?

Probably, providing the renegade Democrats who supported Thurmond or Wallace returned to their traditional party because they disliked Dewey more than Truman. Thurmond won 39 electoral votes and the Southern states of Alabama, Louisiana, Mississippi, and South Carolina. Since Truman carried the rest of the South, he probably would have taken Thurmond's states if there had been no Dixiecrat nominee.

The effect of the Wallace candidacy is harder to analyze. Although he got over 1 million popular votes, Wallace didn't gain a single electoral vote and made a much weaker showing than had been expected. Even so, he may have robbed Truman of the electoral votes of Michigan (19) and Maryland (8), two states in which the combined popular vote for Truman and Wallace exceeded Dewey's winning margin. And New York, which provided nearly half of Wallace's total votes, almost certainly gave its large prize of 47 electoral votes to Dewey because the Progressive Party made deep inroads into traditionally Democratic strongholds.

State	Truman	Dewey	Wallace	Margin of Dewey's plurality
New York	2,780,204	2,841,163	509,559	60,959

DEBACLES

Today's tragedy may be the beginning
of tomorrow's triumph—but tomorrow won't
come for another four years...

Since the birth of the Republican Party, what was the only presidential election in which the GOP candidate did not finish either first or second?

In 1912, when two Republican Presidents ran against each other, and a former professor beat them both! When Theodore Roosevelt decided not to run for another term in 1908, he picked a close friend as his successor, Secretary of War William H. Taft. But Roosevelt was disappointed in Taft's performance as President and wanted the job back for himself.

So in 1912 Roosevelt tossed his hat in the Republican ring and won nine state primaries to Taft's one. When the GOP convention opened, Teddy was clearly the people's choice, but Taft was the favorite of the Old Guard and had the incumbent's advantage of controlling the party machinery. When the Taft forces refused to seat some disputed delegations that were pledged to T.R., Roosevelt's nearly fanatical supporters furiously charged that their idol had been robbed. Rather than accept the convention's verdict and unite behind the Republican nominee, the Roosevelt faction stormed out of the convention and later helped Teddy win the nomination of the Progressive ("Bull Moose") Party.

In the meantime, the Democrats were enjoying the Taft-Roosevelt struggle and nominating Governor Woodrow Wilson of New Jersey, who formerly had been a Princeton professor and later the president of that university. The Democrats boasted that the bitter division within the Republican Party would give them their best shot at the presidency since Grover Cleveland left the White House in 1897.

As anticipated, Roosevelt ran a strong race, finishing second to Wilson in both popular votes and electoral votes. He took six states, including Pennsylvania, Michigan, and California, and his total of 88 electoral votes still holds the record for third-party candidates (George Wallace got 46 electoral votes in 1968).

Taft finished a dismal third, carrying only two states—Utah and Vermont, with a total of eight electoral votes. He didn't even take New Hampshire, which had gone Republican in every presidential election since the GOP was born. (When New Hampshire doesn't go Republican, the party is in deep trouble; no Republican nominee has ever lost New Hampshire and won the presidency.)

Since Roosevelt and Taft together outpolled Wilson by over 1,300,000 votes, it seems likely that if Taft had not been a contender, Teddy would have won the election easily. But this isn't a certainty because the Democratic Party was in the midst of a growth spurt and in 1910 had gained control of the House of Representatives for the first time since 1892. To further complicate the 1912 election a fourth-party candidate, Socialist Eugene V. Debs, polled over 900,000 votes.

1912 Election	% of popular vote	Electoral votes
Woodrow Wilson (D)	41.84	435
Theodore Roosevelt (P)	27.39	88
William H. Taft (R)	23.18	8
Eugene V. Debs (S)	5.99	0

In the 1912 election what state gave the Socialist candidate more than 20 votes for every vote that the Republican candidate won?

This happened in California. Also notice from the figures below that Roosevelt defeated Wilson by a scant 174 votes out of 567,046 cast for the two candidates.

State	Wilson	Roosevelt	Taft	Debs
California	283,436	283,610	3,847	79,201

In which of their four losses to Franklin D. Roosevelt did the Republicans run their best race?

When Roosevelt ran for his fourth term in 1944, the Republicans made their strongest showing, but FDR still managed to win handily in both popular votes and electoral votes.

The Roosevelt years were thoroughly frustrating to the GOP. In 1932 the Republicans nominated an incumbent with a record of impeccable integrity (Herbert Hoover). Four years later they gave the nod to a conservative governor from the Midwest (Alfred M. Landon). In 1940 they supported a homespun Hoosier with a rumpled appearance and a raspy voice (Wendell Willkie). And in 1944 they turned to the Eastern Establishment for a dapper New York governor with a proven record as a spectacular vote-getter in the nation's largest state (Thomas E. Dewey). But no matter what type of presidential candidate was nominated, the Republicans were bowled over by the indomitable FDR.

The Roosevelt Reign

1932 Election	% of popular vote	Electoral votes
Franklin D. Roosevelt (D)	57.42	472
Herbert Hoover (R)	39.64	59

1936 Election	% of popular vote	Electoral votes
Franklin D. Roosevelt (D)	60.79	523
Alfred M. Landon (R)	36.54	8

The Roosevelt Reign *(continued)*

1940 Election	% of popular vote	Electoral votes
Franklin D. Roosevelt (D)	54.70	449
Wendell Willkie (R)	44.82	82

1944 Election	% of popular vote	Electoral votes
Franklin D. Roosevelt (D)	53.39	432
Thomas E. Dewey (R)	45.89	99

Since Eisenhower's tenure in the White House only one Republican presidential nominee has been defeated by a landslide. Who was he?

Senator Barry Goldwater of Arizona, who ran against President Lyndon B. Johnson in 1964. Conservatives praised Goldwater for his courage to speak candidly about his beliefs, even though some of these beliefs were unpopular with large numbers of Americans. Liberals labeled Goldwater an "extremist" and convinced many moderates that he was too radically conservative to send to the White House. Moreover, the 1964 election occurred before the escalation of the Vietnam War, and President Johnson was at the peak of his popularity.

Goldwater suffered a staggering defeat at the polls. Except for his native Arizona, he carried only five states, all in the Deep South. And Lyndon Johnson's 61.05 percent of the popular vote was the highest percent ever attained by a Democratic presidential nominee, even surpassing the previous record set by Franklin D. Roosevelt in the 1936 campaign.

1964 Election	% of popular vote	Electoral votes
Lyndon B. Johnson (D)	61.05	486
Barry Goldwater (R)	38.47	52

PAST LEADERS
IN CONGRESS

When Abraham Lincoln and Stephen A. Douglas had their famous debates, they were competing for what office?

These debates occurred in 1858 when Douglas, the Democratic incumbent, and Lincoln, the Republican challenger, were running for a Senate seat in Illinois. Douglas won reelection, but Lincoln's performance in the debates brought him national attention and served as a springboard for his successful presidential campaign two years later.

During the Reconstruction period (1865-76), what Republican in the House led the campaign to provide civil rights for blacks?

Representative Thaddeus Stevens of Pennsylvania. He vigorously supported the 13th Amendment (1865) to abolish slavery and the 14th Amendment (1868), which gave citizenship to blacks and provided a bulwark against the possible tyranny of state governments. Stevens also helped formulate the 15th Amendment (1870) to give the vote to black males, but this amendment was not ratified until two years after his death.

What Republican led this same fight in the Senate?

Charles Sumner of Massachusetts was Stevens' counterpart in the Senate during the Reconstruction period. Part of Sumner's intense opposition to Southern slaveholders grew out of a brutal incident that occurred in 1856. Senator Sumner had made a scathing speech denouncing Southern Senator Andrew Butler's defense of slavery. Three days later Congressman Preston Brooks, a nephew of Butler's, confronted Sumner in the Senate chamber and beat him mercilessly with a cane. Sumner was nearly killed, and his recovery was so slow that nearly three years passed before he could return to the Senate.

During the Reconstruction period why did the Radical Republicans in Congress want to impeach President Andrew Johnson?

The Radical Republicans were determined to remove Andrew Johnson from the White House because they felt his Reconstruction policies were too lenient on the defeated South and did not guarantee civil rights for the freed blacks.

How did the Radical Republicans provide the legal grounds for impeaching (indicting) President Andrew Johnson?

In 1867 the Radical Republicans pushed through Congress the Tenure-of-Office Act, which they felt certain President Johnson would disobey. This ludicrous law forbade the President from removing without the consent of the Senate all officeholders whose appointments had required confirmation by that body.

A key figure in the plot to get rid of the President was Secretary of War Edwin M. Stanton, a holdover from Lincoln's Cabinet, whose conduct toward Johnson was arrogant, deceitful, and insubordinate. When the President asked for his resignation, Stanton (goaded on by the Radical Republicans) refused to step down. So President Johnson dismissed Stanton without getting the consent of the Senate, thus defying the Tenure-of-Office Act and setting the stage for his own impeachment trial.

How did seven courageous Republican senators incur the wrath of their party leaders and their own constituents during the impeachment trial?

They all voted "not guilty" on the impeachment charges. If any one of the seven had voted "guilty," this would have provided the two-thirds majority needed for conviction. These seven Republicans voted to acquit Andrew Johnson not because they supported his Reconstruction policies (which all of them opposed) but because they felt the Tenure-of-Office Act was an unfair trap and the President had committed no impeachable offense.

Who were these seven Republican senators who dared to vote their own consciences?

They were Senators William P. Fessenden of Maine, Joseph Fowler of Tennessee, James W. Grimes of Iowa, John B. Henderson of Missouri, Edmund Ross of Kansas, Lyman Trumbull of Illinois, and Peter Van Winkle of West Virginia. Senator Grimes suffered a paralytic stroke two days before the vote was taken, but he left his sick bed and was carried by four men into the Senate chamber. There he staggered to his feet to answer the roll-call vote and in a firm voice called out "not guilty."

What happened to the political careers of these seven senators?

Not one of them was reelected to the Senate.

What important precedent was set when Andrew Johnson was found innocent of the impeachment charges?

The precedent that a President is not the pawn of Congress and cannot be removed from office merely because he holds views or pursues policies that are unpopular with many members of Congress.

What senator would have become President if Andrew Johnson had been found guilty in his impeachment trial?

Since the office of Vice-President was vacant, the President *pro tempore* of the Senate, Benjamin Wade of Ohio, would have become President if Johnson had been convicted. The present line of succession to the presidency, which calls for the Speaker of the House to become President if there is no Vice-President, was enacted in Congress in 1947. But the chance of this ever happening was greatly reduced by the 25th Amendment (1967), which makes it possible for the President to nominate a new Vice-President whenever there is a vacancy in that office.

Did the first black senators and congressmen come from the North or the South?

They came from the South during the Reconstruction period

when the federal government ruled the South as five military districts and insisted that black males be permitted to vote. The first two black senators were Republicans elected from Mississippi. Hiram R. Revels, a freed slave, entered the Senate in 1870 and, ironically, filled the seat once held by Jefferson Davis, president of the Confederacy. Blanche K. Bruce, the second black senator, served from 1875 to 1881 and introduced several bills to improve the treatment of minority groups. During the Reconstruction period 14 blacks were elected to the House of Representatives. After 1876, when the federal government relaxed its control over the South, the state governments in the South circumvented the rights of blacks to vote or hold office.

After Senator Bruce's term expired in 1881, how many years passed before the next black was elected to the Senate?

Eighty-five years passed before another black, Massachusetts Republican Edward Brooke, was elected to the Senate in 1966. Brooke served 12 years but was defeated in his bid for a third Senate term by Democrat Paul Tsongas in 1978.

Who was the first Northern black to be elected to the House of Representatives?

Republican Oscar DePriest of Illinois, who was elected to the House in 1928.

Why was Republican Robert M. LaFollette considered a maverick when he served in Congress?

Robert M. LaFollette of Wisconsin, nicknamed "Fighting Bob" because of his aggressive tactics, frequently took stands in Congress that were unpopular with the Republican leadership. He opposed the high Payne-Aldrich Tariff of 1909, the renomination of President Taft in 1912, American entry into World War I, and the drafting of soldiers in that war. Senator LaFollette helped organize the National Progressive Republican League in 1911, and the following year he sought the presidential nomination on the Progressive ticket. But LaFollette suffered a nervous breakdown, and the Progressive nomination went to former President Theodore Roosevelt instead. Twelve years later LaFollette did run for the presidency as a Progressive and polled nearly 5 million votes.

"Fighting Bob" was instrumental in the passage of laws to restrict the working hours of railroad employees, to end the exploitation of merchant seamen, to extend the suffrage to women, and to reform railroad ratemaking. He also was prominent in the movement to prevent the United States from joining the League of Nations.

LaFollette served in the House from 1885 to 1891, as governor of Wisconsin from 1901 to 1906 (when he pioneered the direct primary election for nominating candidates), and in the Senate from 1906 until his death in 1925.

Was Robert M. LaFollette, Jr. also a maverick, like his father?

Yes. After "Fighting Bob's" death in 1925, Robert M. LaFollette, Jr. was elected to the Senate as a Republican, and he too played the role of a maverick. The younger LaFollette fought President Hoover's Depression policies and later supported most of President Roosevelt's New Deal measures. On some issues he was even more liberal than FDR, supporting government ownership of public utilities, munitions factories, and railroads. LaFollette stayed in the Senate nearly a quarter-century, until he lost the 1946 Republican Senate primary to Joseph R. McCarthy.

Who was the first woman elected to the House of Representatives?

Republican Jeanette Rankin of Montana was elected to the House of Representatives in 1916. She served one term and then ran for the Senate, losing in a close primary election by about 1,700 votes. More than two decades later Rankin again was elected to the House, where she served from 1941 to 1943.

What causes did Representative Rankin champion?

Shortly after her first election to the House, Jeanette Rankin announced, "I will not only represent the women of Montana, but also the women of the country, and I have plenty of work cut out for me." She cosponsored a constitutional amendment giving the vote to women, which received the necessary two-thirds margin in the House but failed in the Senate. (In the next session of Congress both houses approved woman suffrage, and the 19th Amendment became effective in 1920.) Congresswoman Rankin

also introduced the first bill to grant women citizenship independent of their husbands, and the first maternity and infancy bill
that provided free hygiene instruction for mothers.

Jeanette Rankin is best remembered for what vote in the House of Representatives?

On December 8, 1941, the day after Pearl Harbor, pacifist
Rankin was the only member of Congress to vote against declar-
ing war on Japan. In 1917 she also had voted against the United
States' entering World War I, but on that vote she had been joined
by 49 House colleagues.

Who was the first Republican woman elected to the Senate?

Gladys Pyle of South Dakota was elected November 8, 1938,
to fill a vacancy in the Senate, but her term expired less than two
months later.

What Nebraska Republican, who spent 40 years in Congress, strongly advocated the conservation of natural resources?

George W. Norris. He was a member of the House from 1903
to 1913 and a senator from 1913 to 1943. A firm believer in public ownership of hydroelectric plants, during the 1920s Norris
struggled in vain to secure the passage of a bill to prevent the
government from handing over Muscle Shoals Dam in the Tennessee Valley to private industry. In the 1930s Norris ardently
supported the TVA and the Rural Electrification Act, and he
sponsored legislation to create a "little TVA" in his home state
of Nebraska.

On most other matters did Norris agree with the views expressed by his party's leaders?

Sometimes he agreed with Republican leaders, but more often
he did not. For example, he joined fellow Republicans who opposed the New Deal's NRA, but he cosponsored the Norris-La-
Guardia Act to strengthen labor unions, and most other Republicans voted against this measure. Norris took the unpopular position of speaking out against U.S. participation in World War I,
alleging that the war would only profit munition makers and
financiers. But he voted with many other Republican senators
against our joining the League of Nations. The independent-

minded Norris refused to support the Republican nominees for the presidency from 1924 through 1940.

What senator was the chief leader of the group that opposed the United States' becoming a member of the League of Nations?

Senator Henry Cabot Lodge of Massachusetts, who was the Republican majority leader and chairman of the Senate Foreign Relations Committee. Lodge was a senator for 31 years, from 1893 until his death in 1924.

Was Senator Lodge adamantly against U.S. participation in any international peace-keeping organization?

No. Unlike Senators LaFollette and Norris, who were labeled "irreconcilables" because they categorically opposed U.S. entry into the League of Nations or any similar world organization, Senator Lodge said he could support U.S. membership in the League if 14 "reservations" (amendments) were included in the League charter. Lodge's chief "reservation" was aimed at Article X of the charter, which provided that League members would guarantee the independence and boundaries (by military action, if necessary) of all member nations. Lodge argued that the United States should not be committed to go to war in defense of another nation unless Congress voted to do so. President Wilson would not accept this or Lodge's other "reservations." So the treaty which would have brought the United States into the League of Nations was never ratified because it failed to get the necessary two-thirds vote of the Senate.

Who ran for and won a House seat because she wanted to vindicate the family name after her congressman husband had been sent to the penitentiary?

Katherine Langley of Kentucky was elected to the House in 1926 after her husband, John Langley, had been sent to prison for selling whiskey during Prohibition. She was reelected in 1928 and might have won a third term except that in 1930 her husband, having been pardoned from prison, decided he wanted to win back his old seat in Congress. Mrs. Langley refused to step aside, even for her husband. The ensuing marital fight disgusted many voters who, instead of electing either Langley, gave the seat to a Democratic opponent.

What congresswoman proposed a constitutional amendment that would have required a direct vote of the people before war could be declared?

Republican Winnifred M. Huck of Illinois, who served briefly in the House in the early 1920s.

What congresswoman was the daughter of one powerful senator and the wife of another?

Ruth Hanna McCormick was the daughter of Senator Mark Hanna and the wife of Senator Medill McCormick, the heir to great wealth (McCormick Harvester Company) and to great power (the *Chicago Tribune*). At the end of one term in the Senate, McCormick lost the Republican primary election to Charles Deneen, who went on to defeat the Democratic candidate in the general election. McCormick died in 1925, and three years later his widow was elected to the House.

But the daughter of Mark Hanna was not satisfied with being a congresswoman. She wanted to avenge her late husband's defeat at the hands of Deneen and become the first elected woman senator. So in 1930 she went after Deneen's Senate seat, and in the Republican primary she toppled the man who had driven her husband from office. But her unpopular stand in favor of continuing Prohibition and the huge amount of money she spent on her campaign in a Depression year hurt Mrs. McCormick in the general election, and her Democratic opponent won the Senate seat she coveted.

What Republican congresswoman had the longest tenure in the House of Representatives?

Edith Nourse Rogers of Massachusetts, who served in the House 35 years, from 1925 until her death in 1960.

J. Edgar Hoover referred to what Republican congresswoman as the "mother of the FBI"?

Florence P. Kahn of California, who served in the House from 1925 to 1937, and sponsored legislation that greatly strengthened the FBI.

Who were the only mother and son that served in Congress at the same time?

Republican Frances P. Bolton of Ohio was in Congress from

1940 to 1969, and her son Oliver Bolton represented another Ohio district in the House from 1953 to 1957.

Who was the first senator since the Civil War to resign from the Senate to enlist in the armed forces?

Henry Cabot Lodge, Jr. of Massachusetts (grandson of the elder Lodge) gave up his Senate seat to enter combat in World War II. Following the war he was again elected to the Senate in 1946.

What congresswoman was the chief author of the 1944 GI Bill of Rights, which made it possible for war veterans to complete their education at government expense?

Republican Edith Nourse Rogers of Massachusetts. President Franklin D. Roosevelt gave Representative Rogers the pen he used to sign this bill.

What senator, who served from 1939 until his death in 1953, was affectionately known as "Mr. Republican"?

Robert A. Taft of Ohio.

Taft is best remembered for what actions in the Senate?

A staunch conservative who placed balancing the budget high on his list of priorities, Senator Taft led the Republican attack against most of the domestic policies advanced by Presidents Franklin D. Roosevelt and Harry S Truman. As a result of the Wagner Act (1935) and other New Deal measures, Taft felt that labor had acquired an unfair advantage over employers. So he helped write and guide through Congress the Taft-Hartley Act (1947), which banned the closed shop, allowed employees to sue unions, and provided an 80-day "cooling-off" period before unions could start a strike that might imperil the national health or safety. After World War II Taft was a leader in the fight to end price controls, cut taxes, and limit government spending.

But the conservative senator from Ohio was by no means opposed to all social and economic change. He strongly supported civil rights measures, sponsored public housing legislation, and backed some forms of federal aid to education.

In foreign affairs Taft was an isolationist until the Japanese attack on Pearl Harbor. Following World War II he supported the Truman Doctrine to aid Greece and Turkey against Communist aggression, but he opposed President Truman's policy of neutrality in the Chinese civil war because he felt it betrayed the Chinese Nationalists and was "soft" on the Chinese Communists.

Were all three of these famous Republican senators—John C. Frémont, Charles Sumner, and Robert A. Taft—elected by the voters of their states?

No. Robert A. Taft, who entered the Senate in 1939, was the only one of these three senators elected by the voters of his state. The Constitution states that U.S. senators are to be elected by their state legislatures, and this practice prevailed until 1913 when the 17th Amendment established the direct election of senators by the voters.

Twenty years before Congress passed the Equal Pay Act, what congresswoman introduced a bill that would have made it illegal "to discriminate against any employee, in the rate of compensation paid, on account of sex"?

Winifred C. Stanley of New York introduced this bill in 1943.

What Republican senator from Michigan in 1945 led the campaign to give bipartisan support to the United Nations?

Arthur H. Vandenberg.

By answering the following ad, what young Republican launched a political career that eventually led to the White House?

"Wanted: Congressman candidate with no previous political experience to defeat a man who has represented the district in the House for 10 years. Any young man resident of the district, preferably a veteran, fair education, may apply for the job. . . "

In 1946 Richard Nixon, who had served in the Navy in World War II and then returned to his home in Whittier, California, answered this ad in a local paper. Nixon won the GOP nomination for this House seat and then defeated the favored Democratic incumbent, Jerry Voorhis, in the fall election. This was the same year in which another young naval officer from World War II, John F. Kennedy, also was elected to his first term in the House of Representatives.

What congresswoman was chiefly responsible for the Women's

Armed Services Integration Act in 1948?

Representative Margaret Chase Smith of Maine.

Who defeated Henry Cabot Lodge, Jr., in his bid for reelection to the Senate in 1952?

Congressman John F. Kennedy took over Lodge's Senate seat by defeating the Republican incumbent in an extremely close race. The 35-year-old Kennedy won with only 51.5 percent of the vote; eight years later he used his Senate seat as the base for launching his successful race for the presidency.

What Republican was a playwright, a congresswoman, and an ambassador?

Clare Booth Luce was a successful playwright (*The Women, Kiss the Boys Goodbye*), a congresswoman from Connecticut from 1943 to 1947, and U.S. Ambassador to Italy from 1953 to 1957.

What flamboyant orator from Illinois served in the House for 16 years and in the Senate for 18 years, until his death in 1969?

Everett M. Dirksen.

What positions of leadership did Dirksen hold in the Senate?

Senator Dirksen was Republican whip (1957-59) and Republican minority leader (1960-1969). One of the most colorful figures on Capitol Hill, he was fond of quoting Shakespeare and writing poetry.

Only twice since 1931—in 1947-49 and 1953-55—have the Republicans had a majority of members in the House of Representatives. During those brief periods of Republican control, who was speaker of the House?

Joseph W. Martin of Massachusetts, who served 42 years in the House, 20 as the Republican minority leader, but only four as Speaker.

What Republican woman confronted Senator Joseph McCarthy in person and courageously delivered her "declaration of conscience" against his "campaign of character assassination"?

Senator Margaret Chase Smith of Maine.

What former Republican congressman won gold medals in two different Olympic Games?

Robert Mathias of California, who won the Olympic decathlon in both 1948 and 1952.

Who was George Bush's father?

Moderate Republican Prescott Bush, who was elected to the U.S. Senate in a special election in 1952 and reelected to a full term in 1956.

Did George Bush ever serve in Congress?

Yes. He served as a Republican congressman from Texas from 1967 to 1971. He also ran twice for a Senate seat, in 1964 and 1970, but he lost both times.

What former California senator first won fame as a movie actor and dancer?

George Murphy. He was elected to the Senate in 1964 but was defeated for reelection in 1970 by Democrat John Tunney, the son of former heavyweight boxing champion, Gene Tunney.

After Californians had elected Ronald Reagan as governor and George Murphy as senator, a third former movie star ran for Congress but was defeated. Who was she?

Shirley Temple Black. She ran in a special 1967 primary election in Northern California but was defeated by a more liberal Republican, Paul "Pete" McCloskey.

What New Jersey congresswoman was an early advocate of mass transit and helped sponsor legislation that established the Department of Transportation?

Florence P. Dwyer, who was a member of the House from 1957 to 1973.

In 1962 Democratic President Kennedy appointed what Republican congresswoman to be a delegate to the General Assembly of the United Nations?

Marguerite Church of Illinois, who was a six-term member of the House before she declined to run again in 1962.

Who was the first senator of Chinese-American ancestry?

Republican Hiram Fong, who was elected to the Senate from Hawaii when it became a state in 1959 and served until he retired from office in 1976.

Who held the voting record in the Senate until 1979 by casting more votes in succession than any other senator?

Margaret Chase Smith of Maine. She cast 2,941 consecutive votes before a hip injury sidelined her briefly in 1968. Her record was surpassed in 1979 by Wisconsin Democrat William Proxmire.

What Ohio senator was defeated for reelection in 1976 by the man he had beaten for this office six years before?

Robert A. Taft, Jr. He defeated Democrat Howard Metzenbaum in the 1970 Senate race but lost to him in the 1976 rematch.

What Republican family of Dutch ancestry produced three senators, a secretary of state, an unsuccessful candidate for Vice-President, and a congressman who served from 1953 to 1975?

The Frelinghuysen family, whose most recent officeholder was Congressman Peter Frelinghuysen, a moderate Republican from New Jersey. He became the ranking Republican on the House Foreign Affairs Committee in 1974, but later that year he declined to run for a 12th term in the House.

What former Illinois congressman became White House Chief of Staff and later Secretary of Defense in Gerald Ford's administration?

Donald Rumsfeld.

In 1980 what North Dakota senator was the only member of Congress born in the nineteenth century?

Milton R. Young, who was born in 1897. Young served 35 years in the Senate, and when he retired in 1980 he was the senior Republican in Congress. In 1974, the last time he ran for reelection, Young tried to minimize the age issue by stressing that he was still vigorous and strong, which he demonstrated by his expertise at karate. Young, who was then nearly 77, made television ads showing him splitting a block of wood with his bare hands.

Who was the only Republican woman to serve in both houses of Congress?

Margaret Chase Smith, who spent 32 years on Capitol Hill, serving as a member of the House from 1940 to 1949 and as a senator from 1949 to 1973.

What Illinois congressman served from 1969 to 1979 as chairman of the House Republican Conference, which is the third highest GOP position in the House?

John Anderson.

What young Michigan congressman became President Reagan's director of the Office of Management and Budget?

David Stockman, who played a major role in proposing the budget cuts that Congress enacted into law in 1981.

RECENT LEADERS
IN CONGRESS

Republicans in Congress before the 1980 elections

Who became the Senate majority leader when the Republicans gained control of the Senate in 1981?

Howard Baker of Tennessee. Senator Baker, however, did not run for reelection in 1984.

Who was Senator Baker's father-in-law?

A former Senate minority leader, Everett M. Dirksen of Illinois.

Did Senator Baker have any other relatives who served in Congress?

Yes. Both his father and stepmother were members of the House of Representatives.

Except for the majority leader, the most powerful GOP position in the Senate is majority whip. Who was selected for this position in 1981?

Ted Stevens, who has represented Alaska in the Senate since 1968.

What New Hampshire senator was a commercial airlines pilot at the time of his election to Congress?

Gordon Humphrey, who was elected to the Senate in 1978.

What senator from Nevada was the son of an immigrant Basque sheepherder and did not learn English until he began school?

Paul Laxalt. He and Ronald Reagan became good friends after Laxalt was elected governor of Nevada and Reagan governor of California in 1966. Their close friendship continued after Laxalt moved to the Senate in 1975 and Reagan to the White House in 1981. Laxalt became chairman of the Republican Party in 1983 and headed Reagan's 1984 presidential reelection campaign.

In 1978 what state elected its first Republican senator since Reconstruction?

Mississippi, which sent Congressman Thad Cochran to the Senate.

What Republican is the House minority leader?

Robert H. Michel of Illinois, who was first elected to the House in 1956.

What Hispanic congressman from New Mexico has been a member of the House since 1969?

Republican Manuel Lujan, Jr.

What congressman was a pro football quarterback for the Buffalo Bills and the San Diego Chargers and won the award as the AFL Most Valuable Player in 1965?

Jack F. Kemp of Buffalo, New York.

Formerly a Democrat, what Republican senator ran for President in 1948 on neither the Democratic nor the Republican ticket?

J. Strom Thurmond of South Carolina, who was the presidential nominee of the States' Rights "Dixiecrat" Party in 1948.

What Virginia senator married a famous movie actress?

Senator John Warner married Elizabeth Taylor. (Later they were divorced.)

What Maine senator first gained national recognition on the House Judiciary Committee that considered the impeachment of President Nixon?

William S. Cohen, who was only 33 when he was seen on TV during the impeachment proceedings in 1974. Four years later he ran for the Senate seat that Margaret Chase Smith had held until 1972, and Cohen easily defeated the Democratic incumbent, William D. Hathaway.

What state that had two Democratic senators elevated to the vice-presidency in recent years had two Republicans in the Senate in 1984?

Minnesota, the home state of Vice-Presidents Hubert Humphrey and Walter Mondale, was represented in the Senate in 1984 by Republicans David Durenberger and Rudy Boschwitz.

What Missouri senator belongs to the family that owns the Ralston Purina Company?

John Danforth.

What Republican senator from Oregon was an early and outspoken opponent of the Vietnam War?

Mark Hatfield.

What Kansas senator is the daughter of a former Republican nominee for President?

Nancy Landon Kassebaum is the daughter of Alfred M. Landon, the GOP presidential nominee in 1936.

New York's beautiful Hudson River Valley, home of Franklin D. Roosevelt, long ago fell under the political dominance of what Republican family?

The Hamilton Fish family virtually ruled this wealthy New York district since 1842 and played an important part in national politics, too. Hamilton Fish, Sr., named for his father's lifelong friend Alexander Hamilton, was elected to Congress in 1842, and he later served as a governor, a senator, and President Grant's highly respected secretary of state. Hamilton Fish, Jr., was speaker of the New York Assembly and later a congressman. Hamilton Fish III served twelve terms in the House of Representatives and was known as Franklin D. Roosevelt's feuding neighbor. (At 91 Hamilton Fish III was the oldest delegate to the 1980 Republican convention and a staunch supporter of Ronald Reagan, whom he described as "the best campaigner I've seen since Teddy Roosevelt.") His son Hamilton Fish, Jr. (IV) was first elected Republican congressman from the same district in 1968.

What North Carolina Republican became probably the best known spokesman for conservative causes in the Senate?

Jesse Helms.

What GOP family represented the same Ohio district in Congress from 1938 until 1983?

Clarence Brown, a small-town newspaper editor, served in the House from 1938 until his death in 1965, and then he was succeeded in the House by his son, also named Clarence Brown and also a small-town newspaper editor. The Browns' congressional district includes Marion, Ohio, the home of a third small-town newspaper editor, Warren G. Harding. The younger Brown ran for governor in 1982 but was defeated by Democrat Richard Celeste.

What Rhode Island senator was Secretary of the Navy in President Nixon's administration?

John Chafee.

What elderly senator married a young beauty queen and fathered the first of their four children when he was almost 70?

J. Strom Thurmond of South Carolina.

What Wyoming congressman was the White House chief-of-staff under President Gerald Ford?

Richard Cheney.

What Pennsylvania senator came from the family that manufactures products with "57 varieties"?

John Heinz III.

What congressman and what senator jointly sponsored the bill to reduce individual income tax rates over a three-year period?

Congressman Jack F. Kemp of New York and Senator William Roth, Jr., of Delaware.

What former head of Bell & Howell, first elected to the Senate in 1966, became one of the leaders of the moderate wing of the Republican Party?

Charles Percy of Illinois.

What Indiana senator was a Rhodes Scholar and later was known as President Nixon's favorite mayor?

Richard Lugar, who was formerly mayor of Indianapolis.

What were the unusual circumstances surrounding Texan John Tower's first election to the Senate?

In 1960 Lyndon B. Johnson ran for two offices at the same time—the vice-presidency and reelection to the Senate. Johnson won both elections; his Republican rival in the Senate race, John Tower, got 41 percent of the vote. When Johnson became Vice-President in 1961, a special election was held to fill his Senate seat. Tower won that election and was reelected in 1966, 1972, and 1978. Tower declined to run for another term in 1984.

What Republican woman, widowed at 26, won a House seat in 1978 by defeating Maine's secretary of state, who was a Vietnam war veteran?

Olympia Snowe.

In 1976 who became the first Republican in 48 years to represent his Oklahoma district in the House?

Mickey Edwards of Oklahoma City, whose district had three Democrats for every Republican.

What young college professor, who used an empty shopping cart as his campaign symbol, became the first Republican elected to the House from the suburbs of Atlanta, Georgia?

Newt Gingrich, who was first elected to the House in 1978.

What Oregon senator introduced legislation to compel all states within the same geographical region to have presidential primary elections on the same day?

Bob Packwood.

Republicans who rode the 1980 landslide to victory

How many seats in the Senate did the GOP gain in the 1980 elections?

Before the 1980 elections Republican optimists hoped to pick up five to seven additional senators. But the unexpected landslide brought the Republicans an astonishing 12 new seats. This gave the GOP a total of 53 seats and control of the Senate. The Democrats held on to 46 seats, and there was one independent, Harry Byrd of Virginia.

How long had it been since the Republicans controlled the Senate?

Twenty-six years. On the coattails of Eisenhower's election, Republicans won control of the Senate in 1952 by a single vote. But they lost the Senate again in 1954, and the Democratic majority persisted until the 1980 elections.

When was the last time that the Democrats lost 12 or more Senate seats in the same year?

In 1946 when Harry Truman was in the White House, the Democrats lost 12 Senate seats in the off-year elections.

Did the GOP also win control of the House of Representatives in 1980?

No. In the outgoing Congress Democrats held a huge 274-159 margin (with two vacancies), and Republicans would have needed 59 more seats to control the House. They did not achieve this political miracle in 1980, but the GOP did pick up a net gain of 33 seats to narrow the Democrats' lead in the House to 243-192. Since some House Democrats (especially southerners) were moderate to conservative, the new lineup on Capitol Hill augured well for many of President Reagan's legislative proposals.

How long had it been since the Republicans won at least 33 new House seats?

Thirty-four years. In 1946 when Harry Truman was President, the GOP gained 55 House seats.

When was the last time that the two houses of Congress were controlled by opposing parties?

In 1932, when Herbert Hoover occupied the White House.

What Republican defeated four-term Senator Frank Church, chairman of the powerful Senate Foreign Relations Committee?

Idaho Congressman Steven Symms, with the strong help of the

National Conservative Political Action Committee, ended Church's long tenure in the Senate. For two years conservatives waged an ABC (Anybody But Church) campaign, attacking the incumbent Democrat for his support of the Panama Canal treaties, SALT II, and other dovish stands on foreign affairs. They also accused him of having antidefense, proabortion, and big-government views.

In 1980 what former Democratic presidential nominee lost his race for a fourth term in the Senate?

George McGovern, the Democratic candidate for the presidency in 1972, went down to defeat at the hands of Republican Congressman James Abdnor, who had more conservative positions than McGovern on key issues: federal spending, national defense, government regulations, and a constitutional ban on abortions.

What conservative Republican defeated both a Democratic congresswoman and the liberal Republican incumbent in a three-way Senate race?

In the New York Republican primary Alfonse D'Amato, a virtually unknown town supervisor from Long Island, scored a stunning upset victory over the 24-year Senate veteran, Jacob Javits. In November D'Amato faced both Democratic Congresswoman Elizabeth Holtzman and Javits again, this time as the Liberal Party candidate. Holtzman was favored to win, but D'Amato, calling himself the candidate of the "forgotten middle class," won a surprising victory, partly because his two opponents split the large liberal vote in New York.

What Republican who had been a Vietnam prisoner of war for seven years became Alabama's new senator?

Navy Rear Admiral Jeremiah Denton, who won the Navy Cross and blinked T-O-R-T-U-R-E in Morse Code across television screens during the Vietnam War, is Alabama's first Republican senator in more than 100 years.

Before 1980 no senator from Indiana had ever been elected to a fourth term. Is this still true?

Yes. When young Birch Bayh won the Senate race in 1962

against three-term incumbent Homer Capehart, he admonished Indiana voters that "18 years in Washington is enough for one man." That warning came back in 1980 to haunt Bayh, who was bidding for his own fourth Senate term. The well-known Indiana liberal lost his seat to Republican Congressman Dan Quayle.

What Democrat with the greatest seniority in Congress was swept out of office in the GOP avalanche?

Senator Warren G. Magnuson of Washington, who had first been elected to the House in 1936 and to the Senate in 1944, lost his bid for a seventh Senate term to Republican Slade Gorton, the state attorney general. In addition to his liberal voting record, Magnuson's health and age (he turned 75 on Election Day) were issues that helped Gorton, 52, as he jogged and cycled around the state.

What Republican woman who opposes ERA was elected to the Senate from Florida?

Paula Hawkins, the former chairwoman of Florida's utilities commission, became the first woman ever and only the second Republican elected to the Senate from Florida since Reconstruction.

Georgia was one of the few states that stayed loyal to Jimmy Carter in 1980, but its voters turned out of office what veteran Democratic senator?

Herman Talmadge, who was denounced by the Senate in 1979 for financial misconduct, lost a close decision to challenger Mack Mattingly, a former Republican state chairman in Georgia.

What Republican won a Senate race in Alaska by defeating the grandson of a former Democratic senator?

Underdog Frank Murkowski won an upset victory over Democrat Clark Gruening, whose grandfather was the popular former Alaska senator, Ernest Gruening.

What Iowa congressman defeated the Democratic senator who had been Ted Kennedy's roommate at Harvard?

Republican Charles Grassley, aided by the religious-activist Moral Majority, won the Senate seat held by John Culver, the victim of his liberal voting record.

In Oklahoma the Moral Majority helped elect the Republicans' youngest senator. Who is he?

Don Nickles, who was 31 when he was elected, only one year older than the minimum age for senators set by the Constitution.

Wisconsin Senator Gaylord Nelson first declined to run for a fourth term, but later he changed his mind. Did the voters return him to the Senate in 1980?

No. Democrat Nelson lost a close contest to Robert Kasten, a former GOP congressman who ran unsuccessfully for governor in 1978.

What conservative North Carolina senator was beaten by an even more conservative Republican?

Democratic incumbent Robert Morgan was edged by John East, a protege of ultraconservative Senator Jesse Helms. East is a polio victim and campaigned from a wheelchair.

What former Philadelphia district attorney narrowly defeated a former Pittsburgh mayor in their close Senate race?

Republican Arlen Specter eked out a victory over Democrat Peter Flaherty for the Pennsylvania seat vacated by retiring Senator Richard Schweiker.

The 1974 Senate election result in New Hampshire was contested, so a special election was held in 1975 to determine the winner. Democrat John Durkin was victorious. How did Durkin fare when he ran for a second term in 1980?

Durkin was defeated by Republican Warren Rudman, who joined Gordon J. Humphrey as New Hampshire's second GOP senator.

Who won the North Dakota seat vacated by retiring Senator Milton Young?

Republican Mark Andrews trounced his Democratic opponent by a margin of nearly 3-to-1.

Besides the 12 new seats that the Republicans gained, what GOP incumbents also won Senate elections in 1980?

Barry Goldwater of Arizona, Robert Dole of Kansas, Charles

Mathias of Maryland, Paul Laxalt of Nevada, Bob Packwood of Oregon, and Jacob "Jake" Garn of Utah.

How many Republican senators who ran for reelection in 1980 were defeated?

None.

Who defeated the Democratic majority whip in the House?

A political novice in Indiana, 27-year-old John Hiler, triumphed over John Brademas, one of the most influential men in Congress, who was seeking a twelfth term. Republican Hiler pointed to the high unemployment in Indiana's industrial cities and convinced voters that because Brademas was a congressional leader he should share the blame for the poor state of the economy.

The powerful chairman of the House Ways and Means Committee was another victim of the Republican landslide. Who ousted him from office?

Denny Smith, a newspaper publisher and son of a former Oregon governor, toppled Democratic Congressman Al Ullman, who had represented his Oregon district in the House for 24 years.

The chairman of the House Public Works Committee, Harold Johnson of California, also went down to defeat. Who replaced this 22-year veteran in Congress?

Eugene Chappie, the Republican assemblyman from Sacramento.

The GOP elected four new women to the House in 1980. One of them, Lynn Martin, represents the congressional district of what recent presidential candidate?

She holds the House seat in Illinois vacated by John Anderson.

Another woman became the first Rhode Island Republican in Congress since 1938. Who is she?

Claudine Schneider, a strong supporter of environmental issues.

What former New Jersey schoolteacher won a House seat on her second try?

Republican Marge Roukema.

Bobbi Fiedler won a close decision over ten-term Congressman James Corman in California. What issue catapulted Fiedler into newspaper headlines?

A member of the Los Angeles school board, Fiedler led the opposition to forced school busing for racial integration.

How did a GOP sheep rancher become the first congressman elected in New Mexico on a write-in vote?

Harold Runnels, a Democratic five-term congressman, was so popular in New Mexico that the Republicans did not even nominate a candidate to run against him. But Runnels died in August, and the State Democratic Committee selected as his replacement David King, nephew of Democratic Governor Bruce King. The GOP also tried to put up a candidate, but a federal judge ruled that since no Republican was nominated in the primary, none would be on the ballot. But this didn't stop Republican rancher Joe Skeen. He waged a vigorous write-in candidacy and defeated the Democrat whose name was on the ballot.

How Congressional Republicans Fared in the 1982 Elections

In 1982 did the Republicans win as many seats in the House as they had won in 1980?

No. In 1980 the Republicans had won 192 seats in the House, but in 1982 they won only 166 seats. The Democrats' gain of 26 seats increased their majority in the House from 51 to 103 seats, thus making it more difficult for President Reagan to push his legislative proposals through Congress.

Traditionally, the party that controls the White House loses seats in the House of Representatives in midterm elections. Did the Republicans lose more than the average number of House seats in the 1982 midterm elections?

No. Between 1946 and 1980 the president's party has lost an average of 31 House seats in years when there were congressional elections but the presidency was not at stake. So the GOP loss of 26 seats in the 1982 elections is a little less than the average loss in midterm elections.

**In the 1982 elections were a large number of incumbent congress-
men defeated in their bids for reelection?**

No. Of the 382 House Democrats and Republicans running for
reelection, only 29, twenty-six Republicans and three Democrats,
were defeated.

**Of the 52 freshmen Republicans who were swept into the House
along with the Reagan landslide in 1980, how many were turned
out of office in 1982?**

Fourteen.

**In which state did the Democrats make their largest net gain in
the 1982 House elections?**

In California, where the Democrats had a net gain of six more
House seats.

**Were there any states in which the Republicans gained more
House seats in 1982 than they had held before the elections?**

Yes. In Florida the Republicans gained two more seats, and
they gained an additional seat each in Arizona, Colorado, Mississippi, Nevada, Oregon, Utah, and Washington.

**Did the Republicans lose ground to the Democrats in the 1982
Senate elections, too?**

No. As a result of the 1982 elections, the Republicans held
onto the same majority in the Senate that they had maintained
before the elections. Before the elections there were 53 Republicans in the Senate (plus the conservative independent, Harry
Byrd, who usually voted with the Republicans) and 46 Democrats. After the 1982 elections there were 54 Republicans and
still only 46 Democrats in the Senate. Of the 33 Senate seats at
stake, 20 were seats held by the Democrats, 13 seats held by the
GOP. This lineup remained intact—the Democrats captured 20
seats and the Republicans 13.

**Did any Republican candidate defeat an incumbent Democratic
senator in 1982?**

Yes, but in only one race. Jacob "Chic" Hecht swept to victory
over Nevada's veteran Democratic Senator Howard Cannon, who
was seeking his fifth term. Hecht, an owner of clothing stores,
was virtually a political unknown before this election. His only

previous political experience consisted of two terms in the state senate before being defeated for reelection in 1974.

Did any Democratic candidate defeat an incumbent Republican senator in 1982?

Yes, but in only one race. New Mexico Attorney General Jeff Bingaman ousted Republican Senator Harrison Schmitt. Although he had rocketed to fame in 1972 as an Apollo astronaut, Schmitt was defeated at the polls after only one term in the Senate.

Did the Republicans win any Senate races in which the seat was vacant?

Yes. In Virginia three-term Republican Congressman Paul Trible narrowly defeated Lieutenant Governor Richard Davis for the Senate seat that had been the property of the Byrd family for half a century.

Did the Republicans lose any Senate races in which the seat was vacant?

Yes. Democrat Frank Lautenberg won an upset victory in New Jersey over moderate Republican Congresswoman Millicent Fenwick, who was the inspiration for Lacey Davenport in the *Doonesbury* comic strip. Lautenberg, who helped build a five-man business-machine firm into a company with 16,000 employees that grossed $669 million in 1981, had never run for public office before.

What father-son combination in Congress ended as a result of the 1982 elections?

Barry Goldwater represented Arizona in the Senate, and his son, Barry Goldwater, Jr., was a congressman from California. In 1982, however, young Goldwater gave up his seat in the House when he ran unsuccessfully for the Republican nomination for the Senate seat that was being vacated by retiring S.I. Hayakawa.

What child of another famous GOP politician also ran unsuccessfully for the Republican nomination for the Senate seat in California?

Maureen Reagan, the oldest daughter of Ronald Reagan.

Who won the Republican nomination for the California Senate seat in 1982?

Pete Wilson, who had been the mayor of San Diego for the previous 11 years.

Who was Wilson's Democratic opponent in this California race?

Edmund "Jerry" Brown, who had served two terms as governor of California and had tried to win the Democratic nomination for the presidency in 1980. Wilson handily defeated Brown to become California's new Republican senator.

What Republican member of the Senate Watergate committee beat back a strong challenge from a popular Democrat?

Lowell Weicker of Connecticut, who defeated Democratic Congressman Toby Moffett.

What Republican senator won reelection over a Democrat who spent more money ($6.9 million) on his campaign than any other candidate in the 1982 elections?

David Durenberger of Minnesota, who defeated wealthy Mark Dayton.

If the Democrats had picked up five more seats in 1982, they would have regained control of the Senate. This could easily have happened because five Republicans defeated their opponents with only 51 percent of the vote. Who were the five Republicans elected by a razor-thin margin?

John Chafee of Rhode Island, John Danforth of Missouri, Robert Stafford of Vermont, Paul Trible of Virginia, and Lowell Weicker of Connecticut.

The percentage of the voting-age population that went to the polls in midterm elections had declined in each election from 1966 through 1978. Did it continue to decline in 1982?

No, the downward trend was reversed in 1982. In 1978 only 34.5 percent of the voting-age population went to the polls, but in 1982 the number rose to 39.7 percent.

One of the Democratic senators reelected in 1982, Henry Jackson of Washington, died September 1, 1983. Was a Democrat or

a Republican appointed to fill this vacancy?

Republican Daniel Evans was selected by GOP Governor John Spellman as Jackson's replacement. Evans, who was president at Evergreen State College in Olympia, had formerly served three terms as governor of Washington.

How did the appointment of Evans change the Republican-Democratic lineup in the Senate?

It increased the Republican majority in the Senate to 55-45.

Congressional Republicans in the 1984 Elections

In 1984 the Republicans had to win back the 26 House seats they lost in 1982 to give them the conservative majority needed to pass bills favored by President Reagan. Did they achieve this goal in the 1984 elections?

No. The GOP gained only 14 seats, which meant that the House still would be dominated by liberals and moderates.

The Democrats needed six additional seats to regain control of the Senate. Did they win these six seats in 1984?

No. Their net gain was only two seats, which gave the Democrats 47 senators to the Republicans' 53.

What two Republican senators were defeated in their bids for reelection?

In Illinois Charles Percy, an 18-year Senate veteran, was defeated by Representative Paul Simon, and in Iowa Senator Roger Jepsen was ousted by Congressman Thomas Harkin.

Did the GOP lose any Senate seats in which a Republican incumbent was not running for reelection?

Yes. The GOP lost the Tennessee Senate seat vacated by retiring Majority Leader Howard Baker to Congressman Albert Gore, Jr., whose father had been a senator from 1953 to 1971.

What Republican won the Texas Senate seat that had been held for 23 years by John Tower?

Congressman Phil Gramm. He had first been elected to the House as a Democrat in 1978, but Gramm was a "boll weevil" who supported Reagan's policies, so he switched to the GOP and was reelected in a special 1983 House election.

What Democratic son-in-law of a defeated GOP senator won the Senate seat vacated in 1984 by Jennings Randolph?

John D. "Jay" Rockefeller IV of West Virginia, whose father-in-law is Charles Percy.

The biggest surprise in the 1984 Senate races occurred in Kentucky, where a Republican challenger defeated a Democratic incumbent. Who won this election?

Judge Mitch McConnell, who ousted Senator Walter "Dee" Huddleston by a winning margin of about 4,000 votes out of nearly 1.3 million votes cast.

In 1984 ten women ran for Senate seats, but only one triumphed. Who is she?

Nancy Landon Kassebaum of Kansas, whose huge reelection win may propel her into the front ranks of women considered for the 1988 presidential ticket.

What ultraconservative GOP senator was reelected in the most expensive Senate election in history?

In North Carolina Jesse Helms, the dean of the New Right in the Senate, withstood a strong challenge by Governor James Hunt in an election that cost about $23 million.

Besides the senators named above, what other Republican Senate incumbents were reelected in 1984?

Ted Stevens of Alaska, William Armstrong of Colorado, James McClure of Idaho, William Cohen of Maine, Rudy Boschwitz of Minnesota, Thad Cochran of Mississippi, Gordon Humphrey of New Hampshire, Peter Domenici of New Mexico, Mark Hatfield of Oregon, Strom Thurmond of South Carolina, Larry Pressler of South Dakota, John Warner of Virginia, and Alan Simpson of Wyoming.

In November 1984 who was selected as the new Republican majority leader in the Senate?

Robert Dole of Kansas.

SLOGANS

What was the Republicans' slogan in their first presidential election?

"Free Speech, Free Press, Free Soil, Free Men, Fré-mont and Victory!"

The slogan "Uncle Abe and Andy" pertained to what election?

The election of 1864 in which Abraham Lincoln and Andrew Johnson were running mates.

What did the expression "Waving the Bloody Shirt" mean?

It meant keeping alive the bitter memories of the Civil War by reminding voters that the Southern secessionists were Democrats. The phrase was said to have originated when Congressman Benjamin F. Butler allegedly waved before the House the blood-stained nightshirt of a carpetbagger who had been flogged by the Ku Klux Klan.

"Waving the Bloody Shirt" persisted in what campaign slogans from 1864 through 1876?

"Vote As You Shot," "Scratch a Democrat and You Will Find a Rebel," "The Boys in Blue Will See It Through," and "The Party that Saved the Union Must Rule It."

"Grant Us Another Term" was a slogan in what election?

The election of 1872 when Ulysses S. Grant was running for reelection.

What campaign slogan in 1876 pointed with pride to the clean political record of Rutherford B. Hayes?

"Hurrah for Hayes
and Honest Ways!"

In 1880 when former President Grant tried (unsuccessfully) to be nominated for a third term, his supporters shouted what verse?

"When asked what state he hails from,
Our sole reply shall be:
He hails from Appomattox
And its famous apple tree."

"Grandfather's Hat Fits Ben" was created to help what presidential nominee?

Benjamin Harrison, grandson of William Henry Harrison. Cartoonists in 1888, however, tended to portray Benjamin in a hat much too large for him because he was a short man, only 5 feet 6 inches tall. Another campaign slogan that alluded to Benjamin Harrison's grandfather was "Tippecanoe and Tariff, Too!"

Three times Grover Cleveland was the Democratic presidential candidate. By the third time (1892), Republicans expressed their disdain for Cleveland in what rhyme?

"Grover, Grover
All Is Over!"

(But it wasn't all over, for Cleveland was elected to another term in 1892.)

"The Full Dinner Pail," one of the most famous election slogans, was associated with whose presidential aspirations?

It was William McKinley's promise to laborers when he challenged William Jennings Bryan in the 1896 election.

What were the Republican slogans when McKinley and Bryan staged their rematch in 1900?

"Four More Years of the Full Dinner Pail" and "Let Well Enough Alone."

Republicans were singing the praises of what popular President when they chanted in 1904, "We Want Teddy for Four Years More"?

Theodore Roosevelt.

In 1904 what did Teddy promise the American public?

A "Square Deal."

"Return to Normalcy" was the theme of what GOP nominee?

Warren G. Harding, who was elected President in 1920.

What was the popular refrain when Calvin Coolidge was the Republican candidate in 1924?

"Keep Cool with Coolidge."

What was the prosperity-tinged slogan when Herbert Hoover ran for the presidency in 1928?

"A Chicken in Every Pot, Two Cars in Every Garage."

Why was the 1936 expression "Let's Make It a Landon-slide" not prophetic?

Because the landslide victor was Franklin D. Roosevelt, not Alfred M. Landon.

The two major Republican slogans in 1940 were simple and direct. What were they?

"No Third Term" and "We Want Willkie."

When the first Republican Congress since 1928 was elected in 1946, voters had responded affirmatively to what two-word phrase?

"Had Enough?"

The best known political slogan in the past forty years focused on the man who became President in 1952. What was it?

"I Like Ike"—which often was expanded to "We Like Ike."

"In Your Heart You Know He's Right" was the way many Republicans felt about what presidential candidate?

Barry Goldwater, the GOP nominee in 1964.

What was the most popular GOP slogan in the 1980 election campaign?

"Vote Republican for a Change."

What were the slogans in President Reagan's 1984 reelection campaign?

"Let's Finish the Job" and "Four More Years."

NICKNAMES

While he was President, Abraham Lincoln was a controversial figure, which was indicated by the nicknames he had. What were some of Lincoln's complimentary nicknames?

"Honest Abe," "Great Emancipator," "Rail Splitter," "Homespun President," and "Sage of Springfield."

What were some of Lincoln's negative nicknames?

"Illinois Baboon," "Hairy Ape," "Ugly Long 'Un," "Tyrant," "Dictator," and "Beast."

How did the famous Civil War general acquire the nickname, "Unconditional Surrender" Grant?

When the commander of the Confederate forces at Fort Donelson asked for an armistice in 1862, General Grant replied, "No terms except an unconditional and immediate surrender can be accepted." The nickname "Unconditional Surrender" was then applied to Grant, and it persisted, probably because it conveniently matched his first two initials. Grant's supporters also called him "The Hero of Appomattox" and "Uncle Sam," while his enemies referred to him as "The Butcher."

What President as a youth had the nickname, "Rud"?

Rutherford B. Hayes.

What were some of the nasty nicknames given to Hayes after he won the bitterly disputed election of 1876?

"His Fraudulency," "Ruther-fraud," "His Accidency," "President De Facto," and "Old Eight to Seven" (which was the vote of the electoral commission that handed him the presidency). The puritanical demeanor of Hayes led to another nickname— "Queen Victoria in Breeches."

Who was known as "Lemonade Lucy"?

First Lady Lucy Hayes, who refused to serve any form of liquor in the White House.

What nicknames for James A. Garfield reflected his experiences before he was President?

"Canal Boy," "Boatman Jim," "Preacher President," and "Teacher President."

Who was called "The Dude President" and "America's First Gentleman"?

Chester A. Arthur, who was widely known for his elegant entertaining and his extensive wardrobe, which included 80 pairs of pants!

What was James G. Blaine's nickname?

"The Plumed Knight," which seems an ironic choice, since Blaine's chief political handicap was the charge of corruption.

What were some of Benjamin Harrison's nicknames?

"The Centennial President" (he was in the White House on the 100th birthday of the United States), "Little Ben," "Grandpa's Grandson," "Young Tippecanoe," and "Kid-Glove Harrison" (he was addicted to wearing gloves outdoors because he thought they were needed to guard against infections).

Why did Republicans hail one of their presidential candidates as "The Advance Agent of Prosperity"?

The nation was in a depression during Grover Cleveland's second term, so in the 1896 campaign the Republicans bestowed this nickname on William McKinley.

Theodore Roosevelt was known by more nicknames than probably any other President. What were some of them?

"Rough Rider," "Trust Buster," "Bull Moose," "Hero of San Juan Hill," "Cowboy President," "Damned Cowboy," "T.R.," "Teddy," and "Four Eyes" (an uncomplimentary reference to his poor eyesight and thick glasses).

What nicknames did Theodore Roosevelt give to his fellow Republican Charles Evans Hughes, who won the 1916 presidential nomination?

"The Bearded Iceberg" and "The Whiskered Wilson."

What were Calvin Coolidge's nicknames?

"Silent Cal," "Cautious Cal," and "The Sphinx of the Potomac ."

Who was "The Great Engineer"?

Herbert Hoover, one of the few Presidents who was neither a lawyer nor a military leader.

What was Alfred M. Landon's nickname?

"The Kansas Coolidge."

Harold Ickes, the outspoken Secretary of the Interior in Franklin D. Roosevelt's Cabinet, gave nicknames to two of the Republicans who ran against Roosevelt. What did he call Wendell Willkie and Thomas E. Dewey?

Ickes called Willkie "The Simple Barefoot Wall Street Lawyer" and Dewey "The Little Man on Top of the Wedding Cake."

The affectionate nickname for Dwight D. Eisenhower stemmed from his childhood. What was it?

Ike.

By what nickname was Gerald Ford known?

Jerry.

What was Ronald Reagan's nickname when he was a sportscaster for a radio station in Iowa?

Dutch.

WIT

During the 1980 campaign President Carter said he was "doing his best." To which Ronald Reagan added, "That's our problem."

* * * * *

When the 1984 campaign began, Ronald Reagan observed that eight Democrats were vying for their party's nomination. "The Democrats have so many candidates," he said, "that there haven't been enough promises to go around. Yes, we Republicans make promises, but not ones to be paid for from the public treasury."

* * * * *

"If you can't make the Democrats see the light, you can sure make them feel the heat."—*Ronald Reagan*

* * * * *

"The forms that the federal government requires are numerous enough to cover Washington, D.C. 25 layers thick—and that's not a bad idea."—*Ronald Reagan*

"There is enough fat in the federal government that if you rendered it, there would be enough soap to wash the whole world."
—*Ronald Reagan*

* * * * *

On a campaign bus driving through a New Hampshire snowstorm in 1980, Ronald Reagan told his staff, "If anyone hears dogs barking, it's because the next leg will be done by sled."

* * * * *

During a debate with his GOP rivals for the 1980 presidential nomination, Ronald Reagan declared that wage and price controls had failed since the time of the Roman Emperor Diocletian. "I'm the only one here old enough to remember," he added.

* * * * *

After Ronald Reagan had already acquired enough delegate votes to assure his 1980 presidential nomination, George Bush defeated him in the Michigan Republican primary. "Do you think I'm peaking too soon?" Bush asked reporters.

* * * * *

When Ronald Reagan was recovering from the bullet wound after the 1981 assassination attempt on his life, he quipped, "If I had had this much attention in Hollywood, I'd have stayed there." The next morning when greeting White House aides, he exclaimed, "Hi, fellas. I knew it would be too much to hope that we could skip a staff meeting." When he heard that the other men who had been wounded in the assassination attempt were recovering, he said, "That's great news. We'll have to get four bedpans and have a reunion."

* * * * *

The oldest President in our history frequently joked about his age. When he traveled to his boyhood home of Dixon, Illinois, to observe his 73rd birthday on February 6, 1984, Ronald Reagan said he was celebrating the 34th anniversary of his 39th birthday. "Those numbers don't mean anything," the President said. "I believe Moses was 80 when God first commissioned him for public service." Another time, Reagan quoted Thomas Jefferson's advice not to be concerned about one's age and added, "Ever since he told me that, I stopped worrying."

* * * * *

When Senator Barry Goldwater limped to the podium at the 1980 Republican convention, he was leaning on a crutch because of painful calcium deposits in one leg. Goldwater quipped, "I know some people back in Washington who ought to be using crutches under their brains."

* * * * *

At the same convention Congresswoman Margaret Heckler of Massachusetts was looking for an elevator and asked directions from an elderly man who was hard of hearing. Apparently he thought she was a prostitute and took her by the arm.

"You don't understand," the woman protested. "I'm a member of the House of Representatives!"

"Sure you are, honey," he replied, pulling at her arm. "Your house or my house—I don't care what house."

* * * * *

Jimmy Carter said that ever since childhood he wanted to be President in the worst possible way—and he succeeded beyond his wildest expectations.

* * * * *

"There is not a man in the country that can't make a living for himself and family. But he can't make a living for them *and* the government, too, the way the government is living. What the government has got to do is to live as cheap as the people."—*Will Rogers*

General Lew Wallace, author of the sensational best-seller *Ben Hur*, was selected to write the official campaign biography of Benjamin Harrison. A mutual friend approved the choice of Wallace and said, "He did so well on *Ben Hur* we can trust him with *Ben Him*."

* * * * *

Thomas Reed, Speaker of the House in the 1890s, defined a statesman as a successful politician who was dead. When a House member asked Reed what to say in eulogizing a deceased colleague, he sternly replied, "Anything but the truth."

* * * * *

Alice Roosevelt Longworth made these caustic remarks about some of the politicians she observed during her long tenure in Washington: Calvin Coolidge—"He looked as if he had been weaned on a pickle." Franklin D. Roosevelt—"One-third mush and two-thirds Eleanor." Wendell Willkie—"He has sprung from the grass roots of the country clubs of America." The Kennedy family—"The greatest political party since the Bonapartes." Theodore Roosevelt, her father—"He always wanted to be the corpse at every funeral, the bride at every wedding, and the baby at every christening."

* * * * *

Theodore Roosevelt admitted that daughter Alice was a handful. "I can do one of two things," he concluded. "I can be President of the United States or I can control Alice. I cannot possibly do both."

* * * * *

In 1904 the Democrats nominated a virtually unknown, colorless New York judge, Alton B. Parker, to run against Theodore Roosevelt for the presidency. Their vice-presidential nominee was feeble, 80-year-old Henry G. Davis of West Virginia. A Republican joker described this Democratic ticket as "an enigma from New York and a ruin from West Virginia."

* * * * *

Theodore Roosevelt was annoyed by the tinkling of a chandelier's prisms in the presidential study. He ordered the chandelier removed, saying, "Take it to the office of the Vice-President. He doesn't have anything to do. It will keep him awake."

* * * * *

Good-natured William H. Taft was the subject of many jokes about his huge size. "Taft is the most polite man alive," remarked one of his friends. "I heard that he recently rose in a streetcar and gave his seat to three women."

* * * * *

While Taft was governor of the Philippines, he became seriously ill. Secretary of War Elihu Root sent him a telegram asking about his condition. Taft got the message at a mountain resort to which he had traveled, partly by horseback. He replied that he felt much better and added: "Stood trip well, rode horseback 25 miles to 5,000-foot elevation."

When Root received Taft's telegram, he wired back: "Referring to your telegram—how is the horse?"

* * * * *

When Taft ran for the presidency in 1908, he refused to accept a live elephant as the symbol of his Republican campaign. He feared that the press might draw embarrassing comparisons between his size and that of the elephant.

* * * * *

"I do not belong to an organized political party. I'm a Democrat."—*Will Rogers*

* * * * *

"When I was a boy I was told that anybody could become President. I'm beginning to believe it."—*Clarence Darrow*

Probably Warren G. Harding's chief fault was trusting too much the friends he appointed to government jobs, but he was a kind, loyal man who didn't realize that some of these friends would take advantage of him. His own father once told Harding, "If you were a girl, Warren, you'd be in a family way all the time. You can't say 'no.'"

* * * * *

"I see a good deal of talk from Washington about lowering taxes. I hope they do get 'em lowered down enough so people can afford to pay 'em."—*Will Rogers*

* * * * *

Because of his thrifty ways, brusque manner, and dry wit, there are many jokes by and about Calvin Coolidge. For example, once a society matron who had been invited to sit next to the President at a White House dinner party bet a friend that she could get Coolidge to say at least three words to her. All through the dinner she tried to engage the President in conversation, but he refused to speak to her. Finally, in desperation, she told him her problem.

"Mr. Coolidge," she pleaded, "I've made a rather large bet that I can get you to say three words to me."

The President turned with an icy stare at his frustrated guest. "You lose," he grumbled.

* * * * *

"If you don't say anything, you won't be called on to repeat it."—*Calvin Coolidge*

* * * * *

When Mrs. Coolidge couldn't attend church services one Sunday, she asked her husband what the sermon was about.

"Sin," answered Calvin.

"What did the minister say about sin?" Mrs. Coolidge inquired.

"He was against it," her husband responded.

* * * * *

When someone asked President Coolidge how many people worked at the White House, he replied, "About half of them."

* * * * *

On another occasion the White House payroll clerk personally delivered Coolidge his first paycheck as President. Coolidge looked up from his desk, smiled at the clerk, and said wryly, "Come often."

* * * * *

One afternoon Coolidge noticed Senator William Borah, an outspoken maverick, riding a horse. "It must upset the senator," Coolidge observed, "to be going the same direction as the horse."

* * * * *

Before Grace Coolidge's portrait was painted with her white collie at her side, the artist insisted she buy a new red dress and not wear her husband's favorite white dress that he had selected. This displeased frugal Coolidge, but he surmised that it probably was cheaper to buy a red dress than to dye the dog.

* * * * *

"If you make any money, the government shoves you in the creek once a year with it in your pockets, and all that don't get wet you can keep."—*Will Rogers*

* * * * *

"Blessed are the young for they shall inherit the national debt."—*Herbert Hoover*

* * * * *

During the 1930s Republicans complained that the people on relief provided a huge voting bloc for Franklin D. Roosevelt. Al Smith, who turned against FDR when the New Deal went into high gear, agreed with the Republicans. But Smith said nothing could be done about the voters on relief because "no one shoots at Santa Claus."

* * * * *

A bureaucrat is a government employee who moves in a straight line from an unknown assumption to a foregone conclusion.

* * * * *

As late as 1938 Wendell Willkie was a registered Democrat, so some Republicans were shocked and angered when Willkie became the Republican nominee for President only two years later. Former Senator James Watson, a Republican leader from Willkie's own state of Indiana, said with disgust, "I have no objection to the church converting prostitutes, but I'm not going to invite one of them to lead the choir."

* * * * *

Wendell Willkie owned several farms in Indiana, and during the 1940 campaign he frequently put on his bluejeans and boots to pose for pictures leaning on a farm fence. He felt this would help him win the farmers' votes. But Willkie's farm manager claimed that his boss repeated the act so often that whenever the hogs spotted a photographer they ran to the fence to strike a pose.

* * * * *

On election day in 1948 a grubby old man on the street told a political reporter what he thought about the Truman-Dewey race. "The political experts," he surmised, "are like the weather man. The weather man predicted rain today, and the political experts picked Dewey. There's no rain, and it looks like it might not even be *dewey*."

* * * * *

After Thomas E. Dewey lost the 1948 presidential race, he said he felt like the Irish politician who had passed out from too much drinking at a wake. He was laid in a spare coffin in the funeral parlor to sleep until his hangover lifted.

When the politician awoke, he sat up in the coffin and looked around. "If I'm dead," he exclaimed in bewilderment, "why do I have to go to the bathroom?"

* * * * *

While Harry Truman was President, a reporter asked Senator Margaret Chase Smith what she would do if she woke up one morning and found herself in the White House. "I'd go straight to Mrs. Truman and apologize," she replied. "Then I'd go home."

* * * * *

Dwight D. Eisenhower's definition of an atheist was a person who watches a Notre Dame-Southern Methodist football game and doesn't care who wins.

* * * * *

"There is one thing about being President. Nobody can tell you when to sit down." *—Dwight D. Eisenhower*

* * * * *

"I remember one time when I was a boy in Kansas," Eisenhower told a reporter. "I had a very good friend, and we got to talking about what we wanted to do when we grew up.

"I told him I had no doubt at all what I wanted. I said I wanted more than anything else in the whole world to be a good baseball player, a real professional—like Hans (Honus) Wagner.

"Then I asked him: 'What do you want to be?'"

"He answered, 'I want to be President of the United States.'"

Grinning broadly, Ike added: "Neither of us got our wish."

* * * * *

Barry Goldwater said that Lyndon Johnson was "so power-hungry, if you plug him in the fuses blow."

* * * * *

"I fly only on planes with two right wings."—*Barry Goldwater*

* * * * *

A frustrated wife said to her husband, "You told me that if I voted for Barry Goldwater we'd be in war in six months, so I didn't—and we were."

* * * * *

"My becoming Vice-President was made possible by a grant from the Ford Foundation."—*Nelson Rockefeller*

* * * * *

Do you know the new Democratic dance? It's one step forward, two steps backward, then sidestep.

* * * * *

Comedian Fred Allen once said, "A Vice-President is a person who finds a molehill on his desk in the morning and must make a mountain out of it by 5 p.m."

* * * * *

A reporter confronted a woman during a recent presidential campaign and asked her why she thought more people weren't excited about the election. "Do you think it's due to ignorance or apathy?" the reporter queried.

The woman replied, "I don't know and I don't care."

* * * * *

EPILOGUE:

WHY WOULD ANYONE WANT TO BE PRESIDENT?

Between the time when he was elected and inaugurated, our first President wrote a friend, saying, "My movements to the chair of government will be accompanied by feelings not unlike those of a culprit who is going to the place of execution."

Later, after he had been subjected to enormous criticism and threatened with impeachment, George Washington declared, "I would rather be in my grave than in the presidency."

Washington wrote to Thomas Jefferson: "I am accused of being the enemy of America, and subject to the influence of a foreign country. . . and every act of my administration is tortured, in such exaggerated and indecent terms as could scarcely be applied to Nero, to a notorious defaulter, or even to a common pickpocket."

* * * * *

"No man who ever held the office of President," said John Adams, "would congratulate a friend on obtaining it."

Shortly after his presidential term expired in 1801, Adams wrote, "If I were to go over my life again I would be a shoemaker rather than an American statesman."

"Had I been chosen President again," Adams confessed, "I am certain I could not have lived another year." Adams was defeated for reelection—and lived to be nearly 91.

* * * * *

While he was Vice-President, Thomas Jefferson wrote to Elbridge Gerry, "The second office of the government is honorable
and easy; the first is but a splendid misery."

After he had been President six years, Jefferson wrote to
John Dickinson: "I am tired of an office where I can do no
more good than many others who would be glad to be employed
in it. To myself, personally, it brings nothing but unceasing
drudgery and daily loss of friends."

Two months before his second term in the White House ended,
Jefferson wrote to Dupont de Nemours, "Never did a prisoner,
released from his chains, feel such relief as I shall on shaking off
the shackles of power."

* * * * *

John Quincy Adams recorded in his diary the message he sent
by a friend to the newly elected governor of Massachusetts:
"Give my compliments to him, and congratulations upon his
election, with my hope that he would find the Chair of Massachusetts a bed of roses, which I could assure him the Presidential
Chair was not."

Many years later President Rutherford B. Hayes wrote in his
diary: "Mr. Charles Francis Adams said that his father, John
Quincy Adams, habitually spoke of his presidential term as the
unhappiest four years of his life."

* * * * *

After six months in the job, Andrew Jackson described the
presidency as "a situation of dignified slavery."

* * * * *

"As to the presidency," wrote Martin Van Buren, "the two
happiest days of my life were those of my entrance upon the office and my surrender of it."

* * * * *

James K. Polk wrote in his diary that his tenure as President had been a time "of incessant labour and anxiety and great responsibility. I am heartily rejoiced that my term is so near its close."

On the last day of his term Polk wrote: "I feel exceedingly relieved that I am now free from all cares. I am sure that I shall be a happier man in retirement than I have been during the four years I have filled the highest office. . . ." (Three months later Polk was dead, chiefly because he had overworked in the White House.)

* * * * *

When Franklin Pierce became President his close friend, author Nathaniel Hawthorne, sent him this message: "I pity you—indeed I do, from the bottom of my heart."

* * * * *

As he left the White House on March 4, 1861, James Buchanan said to the new President, Abraham Lincoln, "If you are as happy, my dear sir, on entering this house, as I am in leaving it and returning home, you are the happiest man in this country."

* * * * *

"If to be the head of hell is as hard as what I have to undergo here," President Lincoln said, "I could find it in my heart to pity Satan himself."

When a friend asked Honest Abe how it felt to be President, Lincoln thought a moment and then replied, "I feel like the man who was tarred and feathered and ridden out of town on a rail. To the man who asked him how he liked it, he said, 'If it wasn't for the honor of the thing, I'd rather walk.'"

* * * * *

"Nobody ever left the presidency with less regret, less disappointment, fewer heartburnings, or any general content with the result of his term (in his own heart, I mean) than I do."— *Rutherford B. Hayes*

* * * * *

The endless flood of eager office-seekers caused President James A. Garfield to exclaim, "My God! What is there in this place that a man should ever want to get into it." (Ironically, one of these office-seekers assassinated Garfield, who died less than seven months after his inauguration.)

* * * * *

Shortly before Grover Cleveland began his second term in the White House, he wrote: "I look upon the next four years to come as a self-inflicted penance for the good of the country. I see no pleasure in it."

Midway through his second term Cleveland observed, "These are days of special perplexity and depression, and the path of public duty is unusually rugged."

As his second term neared its end, Cleveland declared: "I am tired of abuses. I am going to know how it feels to be really a sovereign, for that every American citizen is."

* * * * *

"There has never been an hour since I left the White House that I have felt a wish to return to it."—*Benjamin Harrison*

* * * * *

"I have had enough of it, heaven knows!" exclaimed President William McKinley. "I have had all the honor there is in this place, and have had responsibilities enough to kill any man."

* * * * *

"Politics, when I am in it," confided William H. Taft, "makes me sick."

Taft never pretended to enjoy the presidency, and with complete sincerity he said, "The nearer I get to the inauguration of my successor, the greater the relief I feel."

* * * * *

Woodrow Wilson declared, "The President must have the constitution of an athlete, the patience of a mother, the endurance of an early Christian."

"There are blessed intervals," Wilson sighed, "when I forget by one means or another that I am President of the United States."

* * * * *

Warren G. Harding pathetically admitted, "I am not fit for this office and never should have been here." On another occasion he said, "Oftentimes. . . I don't seem to grasp that I am President."

"I don't know what to do or where to turn on this taxation matter," confessed Harding. "Somewhere there must be a book that tells all about it, where I could go to straighten it out in my mind. But I don't know where the book is, and maybe I couldn't read it if I found it! My God, this is a hell of a place for a man like me to be!"

* * * * *

"I think the American public wants a solemn ass as President," quipped Calvin Coolidge, "and I think I'll go along with them."

After he left the White House, Coolidge observed, "I retired at the right time and am more and more thankful every day. . . ."

* * * * *

In January 1941, Wendell Willkie paid a courtesy call at the White House. Franklin D. Roosevelt, who had defeated him in the presidential election two months earlier, told Willkie: "Someday you may well be sitting here where I am now as President of the United States. And when you are, you'll be looking at that door over there and knowing that practically everybody who walks through it wants something of you. You'll learn what a lonely job this is. . . ."

* * * * *

"No one who has not had the responsibility can really understand what it is like to be President," observed Harry S Truman.

"Within the first few months I discovered that being a President is like riding a tiger. A man has to keep on riding or be swallowed."

After Truman left the White House, he confessed, "I'm glad to be rid of it. One really can't enjoy being President of the greatest republic in the history of the world. It's just too big a job for any one man to control it."

* * * * *

Dwight D. Eisenhower shared the feelings of most of his predecessors in the Executive Mansion. "Oh, that lovely title, ex-President!" Ike exclaimed.

* * * * *

"When I ran for the presidency," said John F. Kennedy, "I knew this country faced serious challenges; but I could not realize—nor could any man who does not bear the burdens of this office—how heavy and constant would be those burdens."

* * * * *

"No one can experience with the President of the United States the glory and agony of his office. No one can share the majestic view from his pinnacle of power. No one can share the burden of his decisions or the scope of his duties. . . . The President represents all the people and must face up to all the problems. He must be responsible, as he sees it, for the welfare of every citizen and must be sensitive to the will of every group. He cannot pick and choose the issues. They all come with the job. So his experience is unique among his fellow Americans."
—*Lyndon B. Johnson*

* * * * *

"What has given the American presidency its vitality," explained Richard Nixon, "is that each man remains distinctive. His abilities become more obvious, and his faults more glaring. The presidency is not a finishing school. It is a magnifying glass."

* * * * *

"Almost by definition, the decisions that must be made in the Oval Office are difficult," Gerald Ford observed. "If they're easy, they're made elsewhere in the federal bureaucracy. Invariably, those that wind up on the President's desk have an equal number of supporters and opponents, an equal number of pluses and minuses, and an equal number of people who will scream bloody murder when the decisions are announced."

* * * * *

"I never see an easy question or problem come to the Oval Office," said Jimmy Carter. "If they are easy, they're solved somewhere else—in a private home or in a city hall or in a county courthouse, in a state legislature or a governor's office.

"And the most difficult ones that are most vital to the future of our country and the entire world are the ones where my own advisers are almost equally divided in the advice they give me," Carter continued, "and I have to make a decision about prosperity or failure, about moving forward or moving backward, about peace and war. . ."

* * * * *

After Ronald Reagan became president in 1981, it didn't take him long to recognize that the American public constantly evaluates the performance of the man in the White House. "It's kind of like the motion picture business," Reagan observed. "You're only as good as your last picture."

BIBLIOGRAPHY

Adler, Bill. *All in the First Family: The Presidents' Kinfolk.* New York: Putnam, 1982.

Aikman, Lonnelle. *The Living White House.* Washington: White House Historical Association, 1982.

Alexander, Herbert E. *Financing Politics: Money, Elections and political Reforms.* Washington: Congressional Quarterly Press, 1980.

Bailey, Thomas A. *Presidential Saints and Sinners.* New York: The Free Press, 1981.

———. *Voices of America: The Nation's Story in Slogans, Sayings, and Songs.* New York: The Free Press, 1976.

Barber, James David. *The Pulse of Politics: Electing Presidents in the Media Age.* New York: Norton, 1980.

Barone, Michael, and Grant Ujifusa. *The Almanac of American Politics, 1984.* Washington: National Journal, 1983.

Boller, Paul F., Jr. *Presidential Anecdotes.* New York: Oxford University Press, 1981.

———. *Presidential Campaigns.* New York: Oxford University Press, 1984.

Candidates '80. Washington: Congressional Quarterly Inc., 1980.

Candidates '84. Washington: Congressional Quarterly Inc., 1984.

Cannon, Lou. *Reagan.* New York: Putnam, 1982.

Chamberlin, Hope. *A Minority of Members: Women in the U.S. Congress.* New York: Praeger Publishers, 1973.

Drew, Elizabeth. *Portrait of an Election: The 1980 Presidential Campaign.* New York: Simon and Schuster, 1981.

Elections '80. Washington: Congressional Quarterly Inc., 1980.

Elections '82. Washington: Congressional Quarterly Inc., 1982.

Elections '84. Washington: Congressional Quarterly Inc., 1984.

Fox, Mary Virginia. *Mister President: The Story of Ronald Reagan.* Hillside, New Jersey: Enslow Publishers, 1982.

Frank, Sid. *The Presidents: Tidbits and Trivia.* Maplewood, New Jersey: Hammond Incorporated, 1975.

Freidel, Frank. *The Presidents of the United States of America,* 9th ed. Washington: White House Historical Association, 1982.

Germond, Jack W., and Jules Witcover. *Blue Smoke and Mirrors: How Reagan Won and Carter Lost the Election of 1980.* New York: Viking Press, 1981.

Graber, Doris A. *Mass Media and American Politics.* Washington: Congressional Quarterly Press, 1980.

Greenhaw, Wayne. *Elephants in the Cottonfields: Ronald Reagan and the New Republican South.* New York: Macmillan, 1982.

Hannaford, Peter. *The Reagans: A Political Portrait.* New York: Coward, McCann and Geoghegan, 1981.

Hoyt, Edwin, P. *Jumbos and Jackasses: A Popular History of the Political Wars.* Garden City, New York: Doubleday, 1960.

Jensen, Amy. *The White House and Its Thirty-Five Families.* New York: McGraw-Hill, 1970.

Josephy, Alvin M., Jr. *On the Hill: A History of the American Congress.* New York: Simon and Schuster, 1979.

Kane, Joseph N. *Facts About the Presidents,* 4th ed. New York: H.W. Wilson Company, 1981.

Kirkpatrick, Jeane. *The Presidential Elite: Men and Women in National Politics.* New York: Russell Sage Foundation, 1976.

Klapthor, Margaret B. *The First Ladies,* 3rd ed. Washington: White House Historical Association, 1981.

Leuchtenburg, William E. *In the Shadow of F.D.R.: From Harry Truman to Ronald Reagan.* Ithaca, New York: Cornell University Press, 1983.

Lindop, Edmund. *The First Book of Elections*, Rev. ed. New York: Franklin Watts, 1972.

———. "A National Need: Music and the Presidents." *American History Illustrated*, December, 1975.

———, and Joseph Jares. *White House Sportsmen*. Boston: Houghton Mifflin, 1964.

Mayer, George H. *The Republican Party, 1854–1964*. New York: Oxford University Press, 1964.

Means, Marianne. *The Women in the White House: The Lives, Times, and Influences of Twelve Notable First Ladies*. New York: Random House, 1963.

Moos, Malcolm. *The Republicans: A History of Their Party*. New York: Random House, 1956.

National Party Conventions, 1831–1980. Washington: Congressional Quarterly Inc., 1983.

President Reagan. Washington: Congressional Quarterly Inc., 1981.

Presidential Elections Since 1789. Washington: Congressional Quarterly Inc., 1983.

Reeves, Richard. *Convention*. New York: Harcourt Brace Jovanovich, 1977.

Roseboom, Eugene H., and Alfred E. Eckles, Jr. *A History of Presidential Elections from George Washington to Jimmy Carter*, 4th ed. New York: Macmillan, 1979.

Russell, Francis. *President Makers from Mark Hanna to Joseph P. Kennedy*. Boston: Little, Brown, 1976.

Scammon, Richard, compiler. *America at the Polls*. Pittsburgh: University of Pittsburgh Press, 1965.

Schlesinger, Arthur M., Jr., ed. *History of U.S. Political Parties*. New York: Chelsea House, 1973.

Shenkman, Richard, and Kurt Reiger. *One-Night Stands with American History*. New York: Morrow, 1980.

White, Theodore. *America in Search of Itself: The Making of the President, 1956–1980*. New York: Harper and Row, 1982.

Wilde, Larry. *The Official Republican Joke Book*. New York: Pinnacle Books, 1980.

Witcover, Jules. *Marathon: The Pursuit of the Presidency*. New York: Viking Press, 1977.

INDEX